Pine Burr 1959

Editor: Mary Lee Chilton

Alpha Editions

This edition published in 2020

ISBN : 9789354043895

Design and Setting By
Alpha Editions
www.alphaedis.com
email - alphaedis@gmail.com

As per information held with us this book is in Public Domain.
This book is a reproduction of an important historical work. Alpha Editions uses the best technology to reproduce historical work in the same manner it was first published to preserve its original nature. Any marks or number seen are left intentionally to preserve its true form.

PINE BURR

Campbell College
Buies Creek, N.C.

EDITOR
MARY LEE CHILTON

YE OLDE ALMA MATER

Professor Ernest Marshall Walker

Dedication

    A college is the lengthened shadow of many individuals who work apart, and yet, together. Each passing year rounds out the impact of their influence. Some are more able, others are more willing, and still others are more durable.

    Professor Ernest Marshall Walker has demonstrated the knack of organizing his life for a maximum contribution. As a teacher of biology, he has stimulated enthusiasm for his subject. As an ordained minister, he has helped in the work of many churches and shared the benefits of his experience with younger brothers on the campus. As a competent businessman, he has demonstrated sound practices and good judgment. As a person, he has accumulated a host of friends.

    In recognition of his cheerful outlook and well-rounded life, his gift of communication, his interest in students and their activities, we, the PINE BURR staff, take pleasure in dedicating our 1959 effort to our friend and advisor, the Reverend E. M. Walker.

Foreword

Your PINE BURR staff of 1959 has tried to make this yearbook a picturamic record of your life at Campbell College. In later years as you turn these pages, you will remember the experiences you had here.

The pictures and the pages of this book added together mirror a year of your lifetime and record for you events and people that have done much to make you what you are.

Yes, here is your college. This is where you met and made new friends. This is where you studied. This is where you thought and prayed and reached for higher, clearer understanding both of man and God. This is where you wept and sang, laughed and worked and loved. This book is a year of you.

We hope that these recorded memories will refresh and help you often in later years as you journey onward into broad horizons.

This is...

Your College...

Where You...

CAME...

Registered...

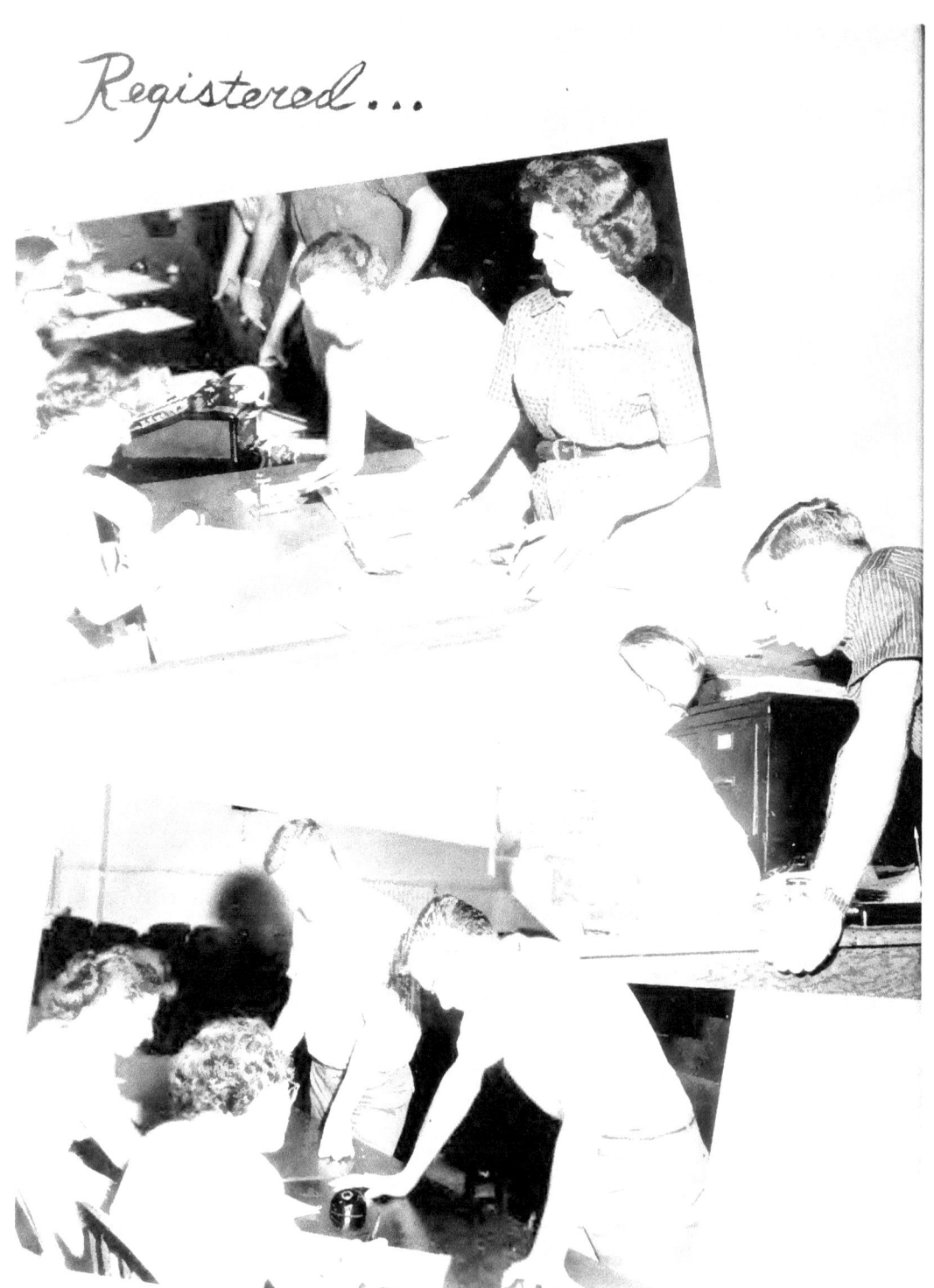

Met friends...

SAW THESE THINGS...

Went to the Carnival...

PLAYED...

Spent Leisure Hours...

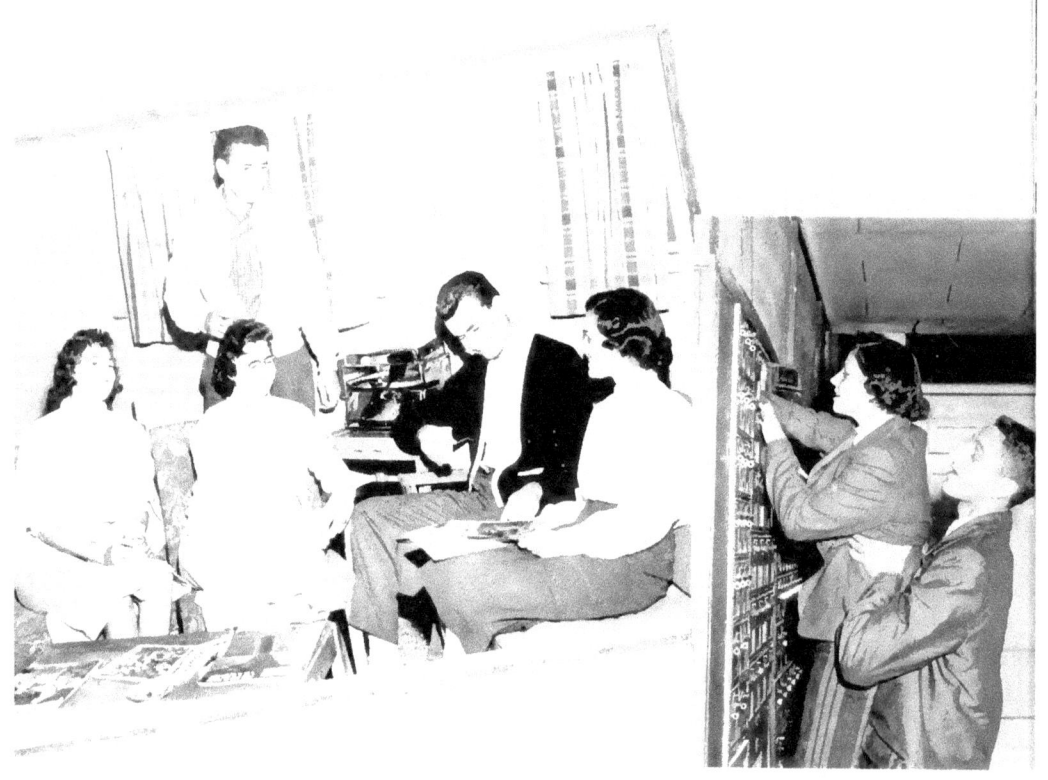

Worshipped

STUDIED..?..

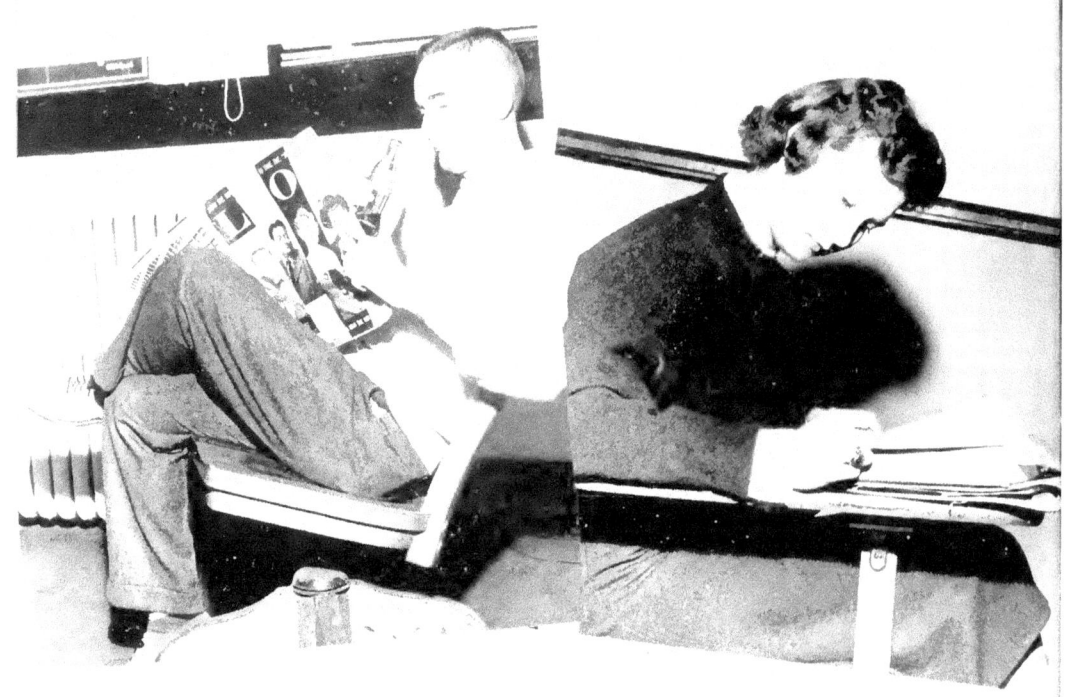

PARTICIPATED IN...

Sports

Freshmen

Freshman Class Officers

JEFF ADAMS	President
KAY WHITE	Secretary
J. D. GORE	Vice-President
RONALD BAIRD	Treasurer
HERMAN PHELPS	Advisor

Freshmen

ABERNATHY, ROBERT SMITH
Fuquay Springs, North Carolina
ABRAMS, JAMES LOUIS
Macclesfield, North Carolina
ADAMS, BILL J.
Angier, North Carolina
ADAMS, JEFFREY LYNN
Newton Grove, North Carolina

ADAMS, LINDA FAYE
Dunn, North Carolina
ADAMS, ROY LEE
Angier, North Carolina
AIKEN, CHARLES LINVILLE
Durham, North Carolina
ALMY, KATHERINE ELIZABETH
Daytona Beach, Florida

AMMONS, HENRY WALTER
Dunn, North Carolina
ANDERSON, GENE RANDALL
Kinston, North Carolina
ANDERSON, LEONARD ELBRIDGE
Enfield, North Carolina
ANDREWS, LEE EARL
Lexington, North Carolina

ANGELL, DON GRAY
East Bend, North Carolina
ANGELL, MYRON MOONEY
Mocksville, North Carolina
ARASTA, MONUCHER
Tehran, Iran
ATKINS, WAVERLY EUGENE
Raleigh, North Carolina

AYCOCK, EDWARD GORDON
Micro, North Carolina
BAGGETT, JOHN DALTON
Greensboro, North Carolina
BAGLEY, WORTH WRENN
Kenly, North Carolina
BAIRD, CARLTON EDWARD
Roanoke Rapids, North Carolina

BAIRD, RONALD SIMS
Roanoke Rapids, North Carolina
BAKER, CHARLES WINFRED
Durham, North Carolina
BALCKMANN, CARL J.
Chapel Hill, North Carolina
BALLARD, CURTIS LANE
Fuquay Springs, North Carolina

Freshmen

BARBEE, JOSEPH FIELDS
Maysville, North Carolina
BAREFOOT, JUDY CATHERINE
Dunn, North Carolina
BAREFOOT, ROBERT EDWARD
Benson, North Carolina
BAREFOOT, WAYLON A.
Benson, North Carolina

BARFIELD, BOBBY GENE
Clinton, North Carolina
BARNES, BETTIE JUNE
Jacksonville, North Carolina
BARNES, RICHARD JOSEPH
Wilson, North Carolina
BATTS, JAMES HOWARD
Kinston, North Carolina

BEALE, CAROLYN MARIE
Lillington, North Carolina
BECK, LARRY EUGENE
Kinston, North Carolina
BEST, BEN GRAY
Dunn, North Carolina
BISHOP, NATHAN MARVIN, III
Durham, North Carolina

BISSETTE, REX AUTRY
Middlesex, North Carolina
BLACKWELL, BARBARA ANN
Virgilina, Virginia
BLACKWELL, BETTY JEAN
Virgilina, Virginia
BLAND, JOHN H.
Rocky Mount, North Carolina

BORDEAUX, GRADY ASBURY
Elizabethtown, North Carolina
BOWERS, THURMAN DAVID
Greensboro, North Carolina
BOWLING, LEE ROY
Aberdeen, North Carolina
BOWLING, WILLIE JEAN
Lillington, North Carolina

BRAUNS, WILLIAM ERWIN
Greensboro, North Carolina
BRIDGER, ROBERT CRAVEN, JR.
Bladenboro, North Carolina
BRILEY, GEORGE HENRY
Greenville, North Carolina
BRILEY, JAMES KIRK
Stokes, North Carolina

Freshmen

BRITT, ROBERT EDWARD
Lumberton, North Carolina

BROADWAY, MURRELL RAY
Kinston, North Carolina

BROWN, LORAINE FRANCES
Mamers, North Carolina

BROWN, LOUISE
Dunn, North Carolina

BROWN, TERRY WINSTON
Four Oaks, North Carolina

BRYAN, SAUNDRA LEIGH
Chinquapin, North Carolina

BRYAN, THELMA JANE
Bladenboro, North Carolina

BRYANT, BILLY MARTIN
Carthage, North Carolina

BUCHANAN, JOHN WESLEY
Broadway, North Carolina

BUCHANAN, WILLIAM WATKINS
Roxboro, North Carolina

BULLARD, MARY FERN
Chadbourn, North Carolina

BURDEN, JAMES ROSCOE
Aulander, North Carolina

BURTON, ORA ECHOL, JR.
Clearwater, Florida

BUTLER, ROBERT M.
Clinton, North Carolina

BUTLER, WILLIAM ADAM
Clinton, North Carolina

BUTTS, JAMES CLELLON
Lillington, North Carolina

BYRD, ELIZABETH LEE
Lillington, North Carolina

BYRD, FRANCES WORTH
Sanford, North Carolina

BYRD, JAMES RONALD
Lillington, North Carolina

BYRD, PATRICIA LANE
Coats, North Carolina

BYRUM, BETTY JANE
Edenton, North Carolina

CALLIHON, JAMES CLARENCE
Clarkton, North Carolina

CAMERON, CHARLOTTE SUE
Erwin, North Carolina

CAMERON, JUDY ERWIN
Kipling, North Carolina

Freshmen

CAPPS, BETTY FREEMAN
Lucama, North Carolina
CAPPS, DAYTON
Conway, South Carolina
CARR, JAMES THOMAS
Carrsville, Virginia
CARTER, ROGER WALTER
Sanford, North Carolina

CARTER, WILLIAM EUGENE
Raeford, North Carolina
CAUDLE, JOHN WILLIAM
Leaksville, North Carolina
CHANCE, ROY LOUIS
Parkton, North Carolina
CHANEY, WILLIAM JOEL
Reidsville, North Carolina

CHAPPELL, DAN MOTLEY
Fuquay Springs, North Carolina
CHEAVES, NANCY ROSE
Spring Hope, North Carolina
CLAPP, RONALD CHARLES
Swepsonville, North Carolina
CLARK, JOYCE ELLEN
Rocky Point, North Carolina

CLAYTON, JOY DAN
Angier, North Carolina
CLEMMONS, IRVING THOMAS, JR.
Leland, North Carolina
CLIFTON, GERALD THOMAS
Faison, North Carolina
COLLIE, ROBERT CARR
Rocky Mount, North Carolina

COLLINS, BOBBY CARLTON
Whiteville, North Carolina
COOK, EVELYN VIRGINIA
Calypso, North Carolina
COOKE, JAMES CONSTANT
Reidsville, North Carolina
COOPER, NANCY GLOVER
Erwin, North Carolina

CORRALES, ENEYDA FUENTES
C. Delicias, Cuba
COTTON, DONALD GENE
Raleigh, North Carolina
CRAWFORD, LARRY JOE
Durham, North Carolina
CREECH, CARSON VASCO
Benson, North Carolina

Freshmen

CREEDE, JEAN
 Greensboro, North Carolina
CRISP, AMOS MANCEL
 Pinetops, North Carolina
CUNNINGHAM, RONALD OWEN
 Kankakee, Illinois
CURLE, WILLIAM EDWARD
 Kinston, North Carolina

DANIEL, CLARA PRISCILLA
 Rougemont, North Carolina
DANIELS, JERRY REECE
 High Point, North Carolina
DARNELL, BETTY JO
 Bolivia, North Carolina
DAUGHTRY, DALLIE PRESTON
 Faison, North Carolina

DAUGHTRY, JAMES ELTON
 Smithfield, North Carolina
DAVIS, ERIC CARLTON
 Raleigh, North Carolina
DAWSON, MARVIN HENRY, JR.
 Durham, North Carolina
DECHENT, ANNE JONES
 Goldsboro, North Carolina

DECHENT, JAMES HOWE
 Buies Creek, North Carolina
DELAPPE, BRENDA RUTH
 High Point, North Carolina
DE MENT, EBBIE RUPPERT
 Oxford, North Carolina
DEMENT, GARVIS MASON
 Holly Springs, North Carolina

DENNIS, CHARLOTTE FAYE
 Holly Springs, North Carolina
DENTON, HUBERT MACON
 Nashville, North Carolina
DEW, JAMES ROBERT
 Whiteville, North Carolina
DIXON, JUDY LYNN
 Benson, North Carolina

DIXON, ROYAL HUNTER
 Clayton, North Carolina
DORMAN, CAROLYN McLAMB
 Dunn, North Carolina
DRAUGHON, ROBERT TAYLOR
 Zebulon, North Carolina
DUKE, ROBERT BYRD
 Conway, South Carolina

Freshmen

DUNCAN, GUY
Nichols, South Carolina
DUNN, BILLIE LOU
Raleigh, North Carolina
DUNN, CLAUD LEE, JR.
Zebulon, North Carolina
DUPREE, ORNETTIE CATHERINE
Smithfield, North Carolina

EAKES, EVELYN LOUISE
Oxford, North Carolina
EARNHARDT, MARTHA GALE
Dunn, North Carolina
EASTERLING, ANN ELIZABETH
Hartsville, South Carolina
EDDINS, HENRY THOMAS, JR.
Durham, North Carolina

EDMONDS, OLIVIA LEE
Hobgood, North Carolina
EDWARDS, JOHNNY BROOKS
Fair Bluff, North Carolina
EDWARDS, NANCY JANE
Princeton, North Carolina
EDWARDS, VIRGIL JAMES
New Bern, North Carolina

ELLEN, BETTY LOU
Jacksonville, North Carolina
ELLEN, PHILLIP IRVIN
Angier, North Carolina
ELLIOTT, MAXINE
Oxford, North Carolina
ELLIS, RONALD GILLIARD, JR.
Raleigh, North Carolina

ELMORE, THOMAS VERNON
Goldsboro, North Carolina
ENNIS, JACKIE O'NEAL
Benson, North Carolina
ERWIN, BETTY WRENN
Lexington, North Carolina
EVANS, ASHBY DORSEY, JR.
Henderson, North Carolina

EVANS, JONATHAN, JR.
Fayetteville, North Carolina
EZZEL, ROBERT LEE
Whiteville, North Carolina
FAILY, ANWAR MOHAMAD
Baghdad, Iraq
FAIRCLOTH, JAMES KEITH
Salemburg, North Carolina

Freshmen

FIELDS, CARL EDGAR
  High Point, North Carolina
FISHER, BILLY RAY
  Bladenboro, North Carolina
FISHER, FRANK WILLIS
  Battleboro, North Carolina
FISHER, JANET LEE
  Lumberton, North Carolina

FISHER, MARY SUE
  Kinston, North Carolina
FLOWERS, CHARLES EDWARD
  Greensboro, North Carolina
FLOYD BILLY EARL
  Raeford, North Carolina
GARCIA, AGUSTIN PAIS
  Havana, Cuba

GARRARD, VICTOR GRAY
  Durham, North Carolina
GARRELL, RUFUS DUKE
  Tabor City, North Carolina
GARRETT, RAY WAYNE
  Moyock, North Carolina
GARRETT, ROY LANE
  Moyock, North Carolina

GASKINS, LAURENS MAXWELL, JR.
  Charleston, South Carolina
GENTRY, KENDALL FRANCIS, JR.
  Roxboro, North Carolina
GENTRY, NANCY LOUISE
  Yadkin, North Carolina
GILBERT, JOHN WAYNE
  Rocky Mount, North Carolina

GOODWIN, THEDA ANN
  Edenton, North Carolina
GORE, J. D.
  Nakina, North Carolina
GOSS, HENRY THOMAS, JR.
  Durham, North Carolina
GRADY, THEODORE KELLY
  Albertson, North Carolina

GRAHAM, HENRY WHITE, JR.
  Sanford, North Carolina
GRAY, THOMAS SCOTT
  Raleigh, North Carolina
GREENE, AUGUSTUS BYRON, JR.
  Oxford, North Carolina
GREEN, CAROLYN AKERS (MRS.)
  Buies Creek, North Carolina

Freshmen

GREEN, ELDON LEO
  Whiteville, North Carolina
GREGORY, MARY FRANCES
  Buies Creek, North Carolina
GRIFFIN, BARBARA ANN
  Middlesex, North Carolina
GRIFFIN, JOE ECIL
  Fairmont, North Carolina

GRIFFIN, JOHN WAYNE
  Fayetteville, North Carolina
GRIFFITH, JOHN ROBERT
  South Hill, Virginia
GRIMMER, HUBERT RAY
  Tarboro, North Carolina
GULLEDGE, MARGARET LUCILE
  Sanford, North Carolina

HADDOCK, ROBERT RICHARD
  Holly Springs, North Carolina
HAIRE, KENNETH ALBERT
  Varina, North Carolina
HAMMOND, CHARLES EMORY
  Linden, North Carolina
HAMMOND, IDA MARIE
  Nichols, South Carolina

HANCHEY, ANNIE ALLEN
  Wallace, North Carolina
HANCOCK, ERNEST VERNON, JR.
  Scotland Neck, North Carolina
HARE, JIMMY MARTIN
  Lyner, North Carolina
HARRELL, BETTY ANN
  Edenton, North Carolina

HARRINGTON, DONALD LEE
  Greensboro, North Carolina
HARRIS, GEORGE CALVIN
  Clayton, North Carolina
HARRIS, MORGAN HOLT
  Washington, North Carolina
HARRIS, REID VICK, II
  Seaboard, North Carolina

HARRIS, WILLIAM SHERROD
  Emporia, Virginia
HARVELL, DONALD HOYLE
  Willow Springs, North Carolina
HAWKINS, WILLIAM LEODRUS
  Petersburg, Virginia
HAYES, GEORGE WAYNE
  Virgilina, Virginia

Freshmen

HENRY, EARLENE GAYE
  Dunn, North Carolina
HENRY, GERALDINE FAYE
  Dunn, North Carolina
HAYES, WILLIAM GREEN
  Fayetteville, North Carolina
HEPLER, THOMAS MONROE
  Winchester, Virginia

HERNDON, ALPHUS SANDERS, JR.
  Durham, North Carolina
HERNANDEZ, RAFAEL ROMERO
  Havana, Cuba
HERRING, RUFUS HILLARY
  Clinton, North Carolina
HICKS, BENNIE WARD
  Nashville, North Carolina

HIGH, CHERRYE LANE
  Middlesex, North Carolina
HIGHSMITH, JERRY MYERS
  Smithfield, North Carolina
HILL, CAROLYN DEE
  Fair Bluff, North Carolina
HILL, SCARLETT LEIGH
  Mount Olive, North Carolina

HILLIARD, RAYMOND GRANT
  Randolph, North Carolina
HINSON, ADOLPH
  Fair Bluff, North Carolina
HINTON, WILLIAM KENNETH
  Zebulon, North Carolina
HOBBS, LESSIE JEAN
  Bunn Level, North Carolina

HOCUTT, BENNY ROYSTER
  Wendell, North Carolina
HOLLAND, HAROLD GLENN
  Morrisville, North Carolina
HOLLAND, PERRY CARLTON
  Sanford, North Carolina
HOLT, LINDA MARILYN
  Albertson, North Carolina

HOOD, EUNICE DORIS
  Rose Hill, North Carolina
HORNE, WALTER WELLS, JR.
  Fayetteville, North Carolina
HOUSE, BRENDA JOYCE
  Erwin, North Carolina
HOUSE, SHARON GAIL
  Erwin, North Carolina

Freshmen

HOWELL, LANNY MONT
Fayetteville, North Carolina
HUDGINS, WILLIAM STONECYPHER
Bayside, Virginia
HUDSON, PERCY CARTER
Dunn, North Carolina
HUMPHRIES, JAMES PAUL
Goldsboro, North Carolina

HUNT, WILLIAM TAYLOR
Grifton, North Carolina
HUNTER, JANICE PEARL
Sanford, North Carolina
JACKSON, JOHN THOMAS, JR.
Dunn, North Carolina
JACOBS, LOUIS GEORGE
Charlotte, North Carolina

JERNIGAN, MARY ANN
Oxford, North Carolina
JOHNSON, CHARLES ASTOR, JR.
Benson, North Carolina
JOHNSON, CHARLES ROCKHILL
Pemberton, New Jersey
JOHNSON, GARLAND HENRY
Jacksonville, North Carolina

JOHNSON, JIMMY WAYLON
Four Oaks, North Carolina
JOHNSON, MAX OLIVER
Benson, North Carolina
JOHNSON, REGINALD ALLEN
Burlington, North Carolina
JOHNSON, SHERRIL LEE
Erwin, North Carolina

JOHNSON, WILLIAM LEE, JR.
Roseboro, North Carolina
JONES, BETTY RUTH
Greensboro, North Carolina
JONES, AMORETTE IONE
Pine Level, North Carolina
JONES, JAMES WILLIAM
Lillington, North Carolina

JONES, WILLIAM LEWIS
Snow Hill, North Carolina
KASHA, ABDULWAHID
Baghdad, Iraq
KELLY, GERALD RIVES
Carthage, North Carolina
KENESSEY, BELA ANTHONY
Kinston, North Carolina

Freshmen

KENNEDY, BOBBY FAYE
Biscoe, North Carolina

KENNEDY, TROY WAYNE
Winston-Salem, North Carolina

KENNEMUR, ANN COURTNEY
Roanoke Rapids, North Carolina

KING, DAVID WALL
Raleigh, North Carolina

KIRBY, MICHAEL BARFIELD
Fayetteville, North Carolina

KITCHIN, MARY ELLEN
Maxton, North Carolina

KNOTT, CAROLYN JEAN
Fuquay Springs, North Carolina

LACKEY, THOMAS LANTZ
Buies Creek, North Carolina

LAMB, WILLIAM STACEY
Edenton, North Carolina

LANCASTER, GEORGE WILLIAM
Lexington, North Carolina

LANIER, HARVEY SPENCER
Leland, North Carolina

LASHLEY, BEVERLY GREENE
Angier, North Carolina

LASSITER, HYLAH CYNTHIA
Potecasi, North Carolina

LEARY, DEBORAH RUTH
Edenton, North Carolina

LEE, BETTY ANN
Dunn, North Carolina

LEE, DONELL, JR.
Dunn, North Carolina

LEE, HOWARD MONROE, JR.
Dunn, North Carolina

LEE, KENNETH MONROE
Benson, North Carolina

LEE, LINDA ALLEN
Kinston, North Carolina

LEE, PEGGY GAYLE
Benson, North Carolina

LEWIS, DEANNA MARIE
Middlesex, North Carolina

LEWIS, JAMES FLOYD, JR.
Clinton, North Carolina

LITTLE, HAROLD LYNN
Sanford, North Carolina

LIVENGOOD, MAX ROBERT
Carthage, North Carolina

Freshmen

LYNCH, REBECCA ANN
Chautauque, New York
McCALL, JAMES EDWARD
Greensboro, North Carolina
McCORMICK, ARCHIE LOCKHART
Thomasville, North Carolina
McDANIEL, ANNA JUSTA
Raleigh, North Carolina

McDANIEL, FRED EUGENE
Fayetteville, North Carolina
McDANIEL, HERBERT ALTON, JR.
Durham, North Carolina
McDONALD, LANCE ALEXIS
Fort Bragg, North Carolina
McDONALD, NEIL ANGUS
Raeford, North Carolina

McDONALD, WILLIAM EUGENE
Lillington, North Carolina
McGIRT, SARAH ELLEN
Maxton, North Carolina
McIVER, WILBUR LEROY, JR.
Raleigh, North Carolina
McMILLAN, DONALD ALEX
Pembroke, North Carolina

McNEILL, ANDREW PATTERSON
Broadway, North Carolina
McPHAIL, WALTER ALFRED
Dunn, North Carolina
MACIOCE, ANGELO
Montclair, New Jersey
MAHARG, JUDITH ANN
Dayton, Ohio

MARE, CHARLES ANTHONY
Brooklyn, New York
MARTIN, LYNDA KAY
Raleigh, North Carolina
MARTIN, TONY GENE
Saint Pauls, North Carolina
MASON, ALICIA INGRAM
Southern Pines, North Carolina

MASSENGILL, ALFRED WILBURN
Four Oaks, North Carolina
MASSENGILL, LINDA RACHEL
Smithfield, North Carolina
MASSEY, BETSY RUTH
Zebulon, North Carolina
MATTHEWS, BARBARA JANE
Sanford, North Carolina

Freshmen

MATTHEWS, CHARLES JORDAN
Nashville, North Carolina
MAXWELL, GRACE DARE
Dunn, North Carolina
MAXWELL, SHERRILL DOUGLAS
Falcon, North Carolina
MAY, HUGH RANDOLPH
Rocky Mount, North Carolina

MAY, JULIAN THORNE
Rocky Mount, North Carolina
MAYO, DAVIS WHITLEY
Fremont, North Carolina
MEADE, HERBERT FRANKLIN
Greensboro, North Carolina
MEADE, JAMES FRANKLIN
Hatboro, Pennsylvania

MERCER, CARRIE LOU
Wilson, North Carolina
MERCER, WALTER KENITH
Kinston, North Carolina
MERRITT, MARGARET ALICE
Burlington, North Carolina
METCALF, WILLIAM HOWARD
Raleigh, North Carolina

MILLER, BOBBY RAY
Benson, North Carolina
MILLER, NANCY IRENE
Beulaville, North Carolina
MILTON, DAVID FLEMMING
Lillington, North Carolina
MINNIS, JENNIE FAYE
Burlington, North Carolina

MINTON, SHIRLEY JO
Suffolk, Virginia
MITCHELL, LORETTA ANN
Aulander, North Carolina
MOLINA, MARIANO AGERO
Durham, North Carolina
MONTAGUE, MARGARET ANN
Angier, North Carolina

MONTALVO, LYDIA
Havana, Cuba
MOORE, EUGENE MOSES
Kinston, North Carolina
MORGAN, CARL ANDREW
Rocky Mount, North Carolina
MORGAN, CLAUDE VANBUREN, JR.
Oxford, North Carolina

Freshmen

MORGAN, ERIC JASON
Spring Hope, North Carolina
MORGAN, PEGGY ELAINE
Lillington, North Carolina
MULLEN, JOEL BENETTE
Raleigh, North Carolina
MURPHY, JAMES IRVING
Zebulon, North Carolina

NACKLEY, FREED WILLIAM
High Point, North Carolina
NEAL, VANCE BROWN
Sanford, North Carolina
NEIGHBORS, JUDITH ALENIA
Benson, North Carolina
NEWBY, MAX FIDDELA
Lexington, North Carolina

NOBLES, RONALD
Richlands, North Carolina
NORRIS, JIMMY AUSTIN
Fuquay Springs, North Carolina
NORRIS, JOSEPH GRAHAM, JR.
Dunn, North Carolina
NORRIS, ROLAND CLEVELAND
Whiteville, North Carolina

NORTON, BETTY LOU
Laurel Hill, North Carolina
OAKLEY, WAYNE DARRELL
Roxboro, North Carolina
OUFFETT, JAMES MERRIMAN
Kinston, North Carolina
OLIVE, DAVID FRANKLIN
Four Oaks, North Carolina

OWEN, GEORGE EDWARD
Virgilina, Virginia
OWEN, THOMAS MICHAEL
Durham, North Carolina
PACE, MAGDLINE
Lillington, North Carolina
PADGETTE, CAROLINE
Smithfield, North Carolina

PARKER, JIMMY SHERRILL
Four Oaks, North Carolina
PARKER, MARSHLON JEAN
Smithfield, North Carolina
PARNELL, ROBERT HAROLD
Durham, North Carolina
PARRISH, CHARLES WILLIAM
Fuquay Springs, North Carolina

Freshmen

PATE, ERNEST VERNON, JR.
Winston-Salem, North Carolina
PATTERSON, CHARLES WAYNE
Durham, North Carolina
PATTERSON, RICHARD CARLTON
Sanford, North Carolina
PATTON, JAMES DAVID
Greensboro, North Carolina

PEACOCK, DON THOMAS
Lake Waccamaw, North Carolina
PEARCE, CHARLIE CLEE, JR.
Durham, North Carolina
PEARCE, PRISCILLA ANN
Zebulon, North Carolina
PENDER, HOLICE EDWIN
Four Oaks, North Carolina

PENNINGTON, EDDIE ROSS
Raleigh, North Carolina
PENNY, JO CAROL
Coats, North Carolina
PERRY, GAYLORD JACKSON
Jamesville, North Carolina
PERRY, JAMES EVAN
Williamston, North Carolina

PHELTS, EMILY FRANCES
Lillington, North Carolina
PHILLIPS, ANN COOK
Goldston, North Carolina
PHILLIPS, CLAUDE DOUGLAS
Raleigh, North Carolina
PHILLIPS, CHARLES LARRY
Goldston, North Carolina

PHIPPS, JEANETTE
Lumberton, North Carolina
PIERCE, HORACE ALHUE, III
Beckley, West Virginia
POPE, JIMMIE RAY
Garner, North Carolina
PORTER, CLAYTON HENDERSON
Lillington, North Carolina

POWERS, JOHN DUNCAN
Lumberton, North Carolina
PRICE, NOVELLA
Bladenboro, North Carolina
PRIDGEN, DAPHNE ANN
Fair Bluff, North Carolina
PUTNAM, GEORGE CARLTON
Rocky Mount, North Carolina

Freshmen

RABON, WAYNE LEVON
Lumberton, North Carolina
RAYNOR, LINDA JANE
Dunn, North Carolina
REDMOND, DONALD SHAW
Liberty, North Carolina
REEVES, RAYMOND WILSON
Westernport, Maryland

REGISTER, EDWIN LEE, JR.
Rose Hill, North Carolina
REGISTER, JIMMIE LEE
Kinston, North Carolina
REID, WILLIAM STANLEY
Rocky Mount, North Carolina
REINHARDT, CLIFFORD JACKSON
Hamptonville, North Carolina

REVELS, BOBBY JOE
Fuquay Springs, North Carolina
RICH, ELIZABETH PARKER
Burgaw, North Carolina
RICHARDS, ROBERT REYNOLD
Durham, North Carolina
RIDDICK, JANIE SUE
Alliance, North Carolina

RIGGS, AUBREY GRANT
Hubert, North Carolina
RIGSBEE, JOHN ALBERT
Durham, North Carolina
RINKER, RONNIE McFALL
Stuart, Florida
RIVENBARK, ROBERT TURNER
Wallace, North Carolina

RIVENBARK, WALTER MURPHY, III
Wallace, North Carolina
ROBERSON, JERRY WATTS
Wilson, North Carolina
ROBERTS, DARREL GENE
Pikeville, Kentucky
ROBERTS, EUETTE MARTIN
Broadway, North Carolina

ROBERTS, MARY ELIZABETH
Raleigh, North Carolina
ROGERS, LINDA DARE
Roxboro, North Carolina
ROSSER, GAITHER DALE
Fayetteville, North Carolina
MALFUNCTION, MR.
Last Year

Freshmen

ROUSE, THOMAS SPENCER
Kinston, North Carolina
ROWE, BOBBY GENE
Kinston, North Carolina
RUSS, JIMMY
Abbottsburg, North Carolina
SALISBURY, PAUL DEAN
Spring Lake, North Carolina

SANDY, HAROLD LLOYD
Buies Creek, North Carolina
SAWYER, THOMAS CECIL
Belcross, North Carolina
SCRIPTURE, MURRAY HOBART
Morehead City, North Carolina
SERCY, JERRY DAVIS
Dunn, North Carolina

SEXTON, RUTH BLAIR
Lillington, North Carolina
SHEPARD, WILLIE, JR.
Wallace, North Carolina
SHERMAN, PHYLLIS ANNE
Holly Springs, North Carolina
SHINGLETON, JAMES RONNIE
Stantonsburg, North Carolina

SINGLETARY, JERRY LANE
Elizabeth City, North Carolina
SMITH, JAMES HUGH
Cary, North Carolina
SMITH, FRANCES RINGOLD
Greenville, North Carolina
SNELL, DAPHNE KAY
Roper, North Carolina

SNIPES, CHARLES LESTER
Selma, North Carolina
SODERGREN, KENNETH WHITE
Emporia, Virginia
SPALDING, H. DANIEL
Landover Hills, Maryland
SPELL, WILLIAM EARL
Autryville, North Carolina

SPENDER, WILLIAM EDWARD
Burgaw, North Carolina
STALLINGS, ARTHUR WHITT
Raleigh, North Carolina
STANLEY, HUBERT CURRIE, JR.
Wilmington, North Carolina
STARLING, MARY STEVENS
Emporia, Virginia

Freshmen

STEPHENS, JOHN LEE
Lillington, North Carolina
STEPHENS, REBECCA ANNE
Erwin, North Carolina
STEPHENS, WILLIAM JONES
Erwin, North Carolina
STEPHENSON, THOMAS WILLIAM
Benson, North Carolina

STEVENS, JERRY HUGHES
Raleigh, North Carolina
STEWART, BARBARA LYNNE
Coats, North Carolina
STEWART, BELLA MAE
Mamers, North Carolina
STEWART, CYRUS FRANKLIN
Lillington, North Carolina

STEWART, THEODOSIA IVEY
Goldsboro, North Carolina
STOKES, HOWARD AUSTIN
Annapolis, Maryland
STOREY, LORRAINE A.
Murfreesboro, North Carolina
STOUT, JAMES BURON
Lillington, North Carolina

STRIBLING, CASPER EUGENE
Tullahoma, Tennessee
STRICKLAND, BERNICE LESLIE
Zebulon, North Carolina
STRICKLAND, JESS WILLARD
Fair Bluff, North Carolina
STRICKLAND, PAUL GRAHAM
Erwin, North Carolina

STUBBS, DAPHNE ANNE
Lumberton, North Carolina
SULLIVAN, VERNON RAY
Selma, North Carolina
SUMRELL, JOHN R.
Harbinger, North Carolina
SWAIN, JEANETTE GAYLE
Ahoskie, North Carolina

SWANSON, JERRY FLOYD
Cumberland, North Carolina
SWEUM, MIRIAM GERTRUDE
Whiteville, North Carolina
SYKES, CLYDE DEWARD
Louisburg, North Carolina
TARLTON, ETHEL LORRAINE
Raleigh, North Carolina

Freshmen

TART, DELORAH MAE
Lillington, North Carolina
TATE, CHARLES LACY
Chadbourn, North Carolina
TAYLOR, JOHN PRESTON
Fayetteville, North Carolina
TAYLOR, STEPHANIE MERRITT
Erwin, North Carolina

TAYLOR, SUE KATHERINE
Zebulon, North Carolina
TEW, CHARLES LINWOOD
Dunn, North Carolina
THAMES, WILLIAM GLENN
Hope Mills, North Carolina
THORNTON, DORIS JEAN
Wilmington, North Carolina

THURMAN, PATRICK COIT
Rocky Mount, North Carolina
TILLEY, ADOLPHUS LINWOOD, III
Rocky Mount, North Carolina
TINGEN, ROBERT WAYNE
Fuquay Springs, North Carolina
TRADER, JAMES HENRY
Annapolis, Maryland

TYNDALL, CARL HAYWOOD
Pikeville, North Carolina
TYSINGER, JERRY RAYMOND
High Point, North Carolina
UTLEY, PHIL THOMAS
Fayetteville, North Carolina
VAUGHN, JAMES GRAHAM
Fayetteville, North Carolina

VEST, JANICE GAYLE
Red Springs, North Carolina
VINCENT, ALTON GENE
Greenville, North Carolina
VINSON, ED LaRUE
Charlotte, North Carolina
WALKER, RALPH EDWIN
Ridgeway, Virginia

WALKER, SAMUEL ARCHIE, JR.
Sligo, North Carolina
WALLACE, RICHARD BRUCE
Cerro Gordo, North Carolina
WALTERS, WILLIAM CECIL
Oxford, North Carolina
WARD, CARR MONROE
Lexington, North Carolina

Freshmen

WARREN, ALLEN JOSEPH
Clinton, North Carolina
WARREN, PATRICIA ANNE
Durham, North Carolina
WATERS, RUBYLENE
Mount Olive, North Carolina
WATSON, BETSY JEAN
Ingold, North Carolina

WAYLAND, BRUCE FOWLER
Wake Forest, North Carolina
WEAVER, DYAL JEAN
Erwin, North Carolina
WEST, ETHEL STOKES
Linden, North Carolina
WHITE, BEVERLY MAE
Youngsville, North Carolina

WHITE, ELEANOR KAY
Elizabeth City, North Carolina
WHITLEY, JAMES ROBERT
Woodland, North Carolina
WILDER, JERRY JAME
Middlesex, North Carolina
WILKINSON, LILLIAN EUGENIA
Durham, North Carolina

WILLIAMS, HOOPER LUTHER, JR.
Clinton, North Carolina
WILLIAMS, ERMA GRAY
Four Oaks, North Carolina
WILLIAMS, SUSAN ANN
Newton Grove, North Carolina
WILLIFORD, PEGGY ANN
Fayetteville, North Carolina

WILLIFORD, SONJA LEE
Maxton, North Carolina
WILSON, ELIZABETH ROSE
Whiteville, North Carolina
WILSON, CAROLYN WRAY
Rocky Point, North Carolina
WILSON, SARA FRANCES
Angier, North Carolina

WIMBERLY, PATRICIA ANN
Lillington, North Carolina
WOMACK, BUCK J.
Broadway, North Carolina
WOOD, BENNY BURTON
Dunn, North Carolina
WOOD, EARL EDISON
Mamers, North Carolina

Freshmen

WOOD, JUDY FAYE
  Dunn, North Carolina
WOODARD, LOUIS HERMAN
  Kinston, North Carolina
WOODARD, MARY CRAIG
  Charlotte, North Carolina
WOODLEY, DORA HESTA
  Angier, North Carolina

WORTHAM, JAMES HOWARD
  Fuquay Springs, North Carolina
WRIGHT, JOE WOODRUFF
  Hamptonville, North Carolina
YOUNG, JIMMIE BRYANT
  Louisburg, North Carolina
YOUNG, THOMAS ALVEY
  Woodsdale, North Carolina

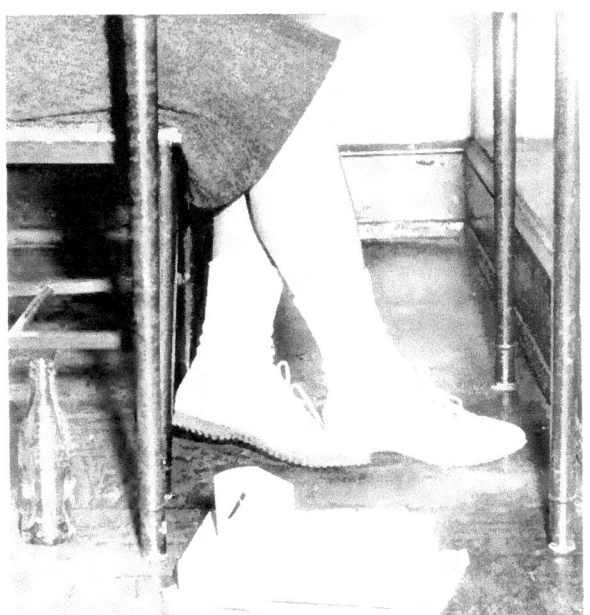

Sophomores

Sophomore Class Officers

GLEN JERNIGAN .... President
JESSIE TAYLOR .... Treasurer
GORDON HARRISON Vice-President
BECKY WEBSTER Secretary
E. M. WALKER Advisor

ADAMS, JOEL RAY
  Angier, North Carolina
ADAMS, JULIAN FREDERICK, JR.
  Raleigh, North Carolina
ADAMS, ROBERT ANCILE
  Clayton, North Carolina

ADCOCK, STARLON WILLIS
  Lillington, North Carolina
ALPHIN, CLARA LYNDA
  Mt. Olive, North Carolina
AMMONS, MARY JAN
  Lumberton, North Carolina

ATKINSON, RONALD ROBERT
  Riverside, New Jersey
AUTRY, WILLIAM SEYMOUR
  Stedman, North Carolina
AVERY, LARRY EARL
  Erwin, North Carolina

AVERY, ROY LEON
  Dunn, North Carolina
BAILEY, CONRAD ZIEGLER, JR.
  Elizabeth City, North Carolina
BAKER, EVERETTE NORMAN
  Broadway, North Carolina

BALLENTINE, JOHN WARREN
Raleigh, North Carolina

BAREFOOT, BARBARA ANN
Four Oaks, North Carolina

BAREFOOT, BETSY LEIGH
Four Oaks, North Carolina

BARFIELD, WILLIAM POPE
Dunn, North Carolina

BARLOW, LEONARD HALL, JR.
Kannapolis, North Carolina

BARNES, LINDA FAYE
Lumberton, North Carolina

BASS, WILLIAM ELWOOD
Four Oaks, North Carolina

BENNETT, MARY ZILLAH
Ash, North Carolina

BERRY, ROBERT CLAIBORNE
Durham, North Carolina

BEST, JOE CEPHUS
Goldsboro, North Carolina

BLAKE, PEGGY IRENE
Rockingham, North Carolina

BLOWE, JEWEL ANNE
Boykins, Virginia

BOGGESS, ANN HOWARD
Havelock, North Carolina
BOND, GRACE JEAN
Buies Creek, North Carolina
BRACKNEY, KENNARD SAMUEL
Hyattsville, Maryland

BRANTLEY, ERASTUS CLIFFORD, JR.
Zebulon, North Carolina
BRIGGS, THOMAS WOODROW
Cameron, North Carolina
BRITT, BETTY ANNE
Lumberton, North Carolina

BROOKS, DAVID EUGENE
Bath, North Carolina
BROOKS, GENE TERRELL
Albemarle, North Carolina
BROOKS, TOMMY GEORGE, JR.
Wallace, North Carolina

BROWN, BILLIE DEAN
Dunn, North Carolina
BROWN, CHARLES FRANKLIN, JR.
Hope Mills, North Carolina
BROWN, DENICE KAY
Lillington, North Carolina

BROWN, WANDA LYNNE
Stacy, North Carolina
BRYAN, ALEX GRAY
Jacksonville, North Carolina
BRYAN, JAMES STEDMAN BLACK
Fayetteville, North Carolina

BRYAN, LOIS ANN
Lumberton, North Carolina
BRYANT, ROBERT SMALL
Buies Creek, North Carolina
BUFFALOE, WILLIAM BRYANT
Garner, North Carolina

BULLARD, WILLIE MONROE
Raleigh, North Carolina
BUNN, SARAH ANN
Wake Forest, North Carolina
BYRD, BILLIE JEAN
Coats, North Carolina

BYRD, BILLY DALE
Buies Creek, North Carolina
BYRD, HUBERT GLENWOOD
Coats, North Carolina
BYRD, NEIL ALLEN
Bunnlevel, North Carolina

BYRD, ROBERT GENTRY
Hope Mills, North Carolina
CAMPBELL, WILLIAM LANCE
Winston-Salem, North Carolina
CARR, EUGENE BRYAN
Godwin, North Carolina

CARR, JERRY THOMAS
Godwin, North Carolina
CARROLL, BETSY LOU
Asheboro, North Carolina
CASTELLOE, RALEIGH ROOSEVELT, JR.
Windsor, North Carolina

CHALLENDER, RAYMOND HOWARD
Pemberton, New Jersey
CHILTON, MARY LEE
Moseley, Virginia
CHURCHILL, JOYCE ANNE
Hyattsville, Maryland

CLARK, GORDON WILLIAM
Sanford, North Carolina
COATS, CHARLES WILLIAM
Angier, North Carolina
COBB, ARTHUR WESLEY
Reidsville, North Carolina

COLLEY, THOMAS JACK, JR.
Camp Lejeune, North Carolina
COLVILLE, HAROLD EUGENE
Bunnlevel, North Carolina
COOPER, DONALD RAYMOND
Cary, North Carolina

CORBETT, FREDDIE LUVON
Selma, North Carolina
COUGHENOUR, RICHARD NORFLEET, JR.
Fayetteville, North Carolina
COURIE, RAYMOND TAFT
Kinston, North Carolina

CRANMER, PAUL IRVING
Pemberton, New Jersey
CRAWLEY, WILLIAM CHARLES
Raleigh, North Carolina
CREECH, BILLIE ANN
Princeton, North Carolina

CREECH, MARION FARRIOR
Warsaw, North Carolina
CROMARTIE, MEREDITH SUE
Dunn, North Carolina
CRUMPLER, VERNON RAY
Clinton, North Carolina

59

DAUGHTRIDGE, JOSEPH GARLAND
Rocky Mount, North Carolina
DAVIS, ROLAND BOWDEN, JR.
Seven Springs, North Carolina
DAVIS, WAYLAND THOMAS
Albertson, North Carolina

DAY, DAVID ALEXANDER
Murfreesboro, North Carolina
DEWBERRY, WILLIS ELBERT, JR.
Baltimore, Maryland
DEWBERRY, GERALDINE MERCEDES
Baltimore, Maryland

DODSON, JERRY DEAN
Mt. Airy, North Carolina
DOUGLAS, DON KELLY
Greensboro, North Carolina
DUNCAN, THOMAS SHERRILL
Angier, North Carolina

EARP, GEORGE A.
Winnabow, North Carolina
EARP, JOE THOMAS
Angier, North Carolina
ELKS, HELEN ELIZABETH
Pikeville, North Carolina

19

ELLIS, JOHNNIE MELVIN
Clayton, North Carolina

ERGOOD, RUSSELL MERRIEL, III
Haddonfield, New Jersey

EVANS, EDWARD ROBERT
Ahoskie, North Carolina

FASTIGE, ANTHONY NICHOLAS
Montclair, New Jersey

FEARING, GORDON BRADFORD
Elizabeth City, North Carolina

FISHER, WILLIAM C. P.
Wake Forest, North Carolina

FISHER, JOHN WHITE
Battleboro, North Carolina

FLEISHMAN, MORTON THEODORE
Fayetteville, North Carolina

FLOWERS, SIBYL WHITEHEAD
Ramseur, North Carolina

FRENCH, WILLIAM WASHINGTON, JR.
Charlotte, North Carolina

FUTRELL, BETTY LOU
Lucama, North Carolina

FUTRELL, ISAAC GERALD
Lucama, North Carolina

GAINES, JOHN ALEXANDER, JR.
Sanford, North Carolina
GARDNER, SUE CAROLYN
Dunn, North Carolina
GASTER, MARVIN EDWARD
Sanford, North Carolina

GILBERT, NORMAN RAY
Greensboro, North Carolina
GILDEN, MYRTLE, KAY
Grandy, North Carolina
GILL, HORACE THOMAS
Bullock, North Carolina

GODWIN, BOBBY D.
Dunn, North Carolina
GODWIN, WILEY NORWOOD
Dunn, North Carolina
GODWIN, WILLIAM JACKIE
Clarendon, North Carolina

GRADY, ROBERT SHELTON
Albertson, North Carolina
GRAY, THOMAS NILE
Fuquay, North Carolina
GRESHAM, GERALDINE FAISON
Raleigh, North Carolina

59

GRIFFIN, ANNIE JO
Louisburg, North Carolina
GRUBBS, SYLVIA FAYE
Burlington, North Carolina
GURGANUS, CLAUDIUS LEACH
Smithfield, North Carolina

HALES, JOHN BRADLEY
Bladenboro, North Carolina
HALL, GEORGE RUBIN
Raleigh, North Carolina
HALL, JAMES OWEN
Benson, North Carolina

HALL, ROBERT HAROLD
Holly Springs, North Carolina
HAMILTON, JESSIE SUGGS
Dunn, North Carolina
HANNON, CATHERINE LOUISA
Henderson, North Carolina

HARDEN, JOE ALLEN
Bladenboro, North Carolina
HARGROVE, WILBUR HOWARD
Vincentown, New Jersey
HORRELL, ADRIAN PHILMORE
Atkinson, North Carolina

59

HARRINGTON, JANET ANN
Broadway, North Carolina

HARRIS, CHARLES TOBY
Raleigh, North Carolina

HARRISON, GORDON MARSHALL
Pocomoke, Maryland

HAWES, REUBEN HOMER
Rose Hill, North Carolina

HOBBS, RODNEY CARROLL
Bunnlevel, North Carolina

HODGES, ROBERT WILSON
Washington, North Carolina

HOLT, RALPH EDWARD, JR.
Durham, North Carolina

HOWELL, DAVID JACK
Raleigh, North Carolina

HUDSON, JOEL BLANNEY
Clinton, North Carolina

HUGHES, ELMOND LEE
Charleston, South Carolina

HUGHS, PATSY ELIZABETH
Oxford, North Carolina

HUMPHREY, C. W., JR.
Kinston, North Carolina

HUMPHREY, CARLYLE PAUL
Shannon, North Carolina

HURST, SARA LOWDER
Jacksonville, North Carolina

HUTCHINSON, HOYT PHILLIP, JR.
Nichols, South Carolina

JACKSON, ALICE LOU
Dunn, North Carolina

JACKSON, JOE WADE
Fayetteville, North Carolina

JACKSON, CECILE KAY
Tarboro, North Carolina

JACKSON, LYNN RANDALL
Beulaville, North Carolina

JAMES, CHARLES HENRY
Elizabeth City, North Carolina

JENKINS, ROBERT HOBGOOD
Zebulon, North Carolina

JENNINGS, ROBERT LEE
Elizabeth City, North Carolina

JERNIGAN, GLENN REGINALD
Charlotte, North Carolina

JONES, BOBBY RAY
Raleigh, North Carolina

JONES, LEWIS ROY
  Oxford, North Carolina
JONES, WILLIAM LOUIS
  Raleigh, North Carolina
KELLY, BARBARA ANN
  Garner, North Carolina

KLUGEL, SARAH YORKSHIRE
  Emporia, Virginia
KUBE, DELORES ANN
  Hyattsville, Maryland
LANIER, WALTER CRAVEN
  Lillington, North Carolina

LASLEY, CHARLES GLENN, JR.
  Draper, North Carolina
LEE, WADE THOMAS
  Four Oaks, North Carolina
LEE, WILLIAM DALTON, JR.
  Angier, North Carolina

LENNON, MARGARET RUTH
  Clarkton, North Carolina
LEONARD, FRANCES ADELAIDE
  Louisburg, North Carolina
LEWIS, KITTY MARGOT
  Bolivia, North Carolina

59

LITTLE, EDGAR LEROY
Durham, North Carolina
LYNCH, ROBERT JACKSON
Apex, North Carolina
LYNN, DANIEL CARSON
Raleigh, North Carolina

McGUGAN, DAVID BROWN
Red Springs, North Carolina
McGRAW, MARY ELIZABETH
Cliffside, North Carolina
McLAMB, BARBARA ANN
Lillington, North Carolina

McLAMB, EDNA JEAN
Wade, North Carolina
McLEAN, RITA PHYLLIS
Dunn, North Carolina
McLEOD, DAVID GWIN
Fayetteville, North Carolina

McLEOD, JO ANN
Buies Creek, North Carolina
MASON, RAYMOND BRUCE
Fuquay Springs, North Carolina
MATTHEWS, FRED LEE
Fuquay Springs, North Carolina

59

MAXWELL, HUGH GORDON
Goldsboro, North Carolina
MAYO, FRANK TAYLOR
Rocky Mount, North Carolina
MEDLIN, GERALD WAYNE
Sanford, North Carolina

MERRITT, BILLY CHARLES
Rocky Mount, North Carolina
MIDKIFF, JOHN WALTER
Mt. Airy, North Carolina
MOORE, JAMES ROBERT, III
Rocky Mount, North Carolina

MOORE, HENRY WALTON, JR.
Hillsboro, North Carolina
MOORE, WILLIAM DAVIS
Hillsboro, North Carolina
MORRIS, JIMMY AUSTIN
Kenly, North Carolina

MORTON, RONALD GREY
Sanford, North Carolina
MOZINGO, GARLAND RAY
Goldsboro, North Carolina
NORFLEET, LEON EDGAR
Smithfield, North Carolina

19

NORRIS, TERRY GOAL
  Elizabethtown, North Carolina
OLIVE, JAMES EDWARD
  Willow Springs, North Carolina
PAGE, FAITH HELEN
  Lillington, North Carolina

PARKER, BOBBY EUGENE
  Four Oaks, North Carolina
PARKER, DAVID WALTER
  Whitakers, North Carolina
PARKER, JO-ANN CREECH
  Selma, North Carolina

PATTERSON, DAISY ANN
  Raleigh, North Carolina
PEELE, JULIAN THOMAS
  Jacksonville, North Carolina
PLEASANT, JERRY THOMAS
  Angier, North Carolina

POE, ALBERT M.
  Durham, North Carolina
POPE, REBECCA ANN
  Coats, North Carolina
PORTER, RAYMOND NIXON, JR.
  Sanford, North Carolina

PRITCHARD, EDWARD LEE
Elizabeth City, North Carolina
QUICK, GERALD GILBERT
McColl, South Carolina
RAMSEY, KADER ROY
Jacksonville, North Carolina

RAYNOR, ELIZABETH ANN
Burlington, North Carolina
REAVIS, JUNE BEN
Fayetteville, North Carolina
RENFROW, HILTON VESTER
Kenly, North Carolina

REUSCHLING, GORDON NELSON, JR.
Portsmouth, Virginia
RIGSBEE, CHARLES STEWART
Durham, North Carolina
ROBERTS, CAROL JOANNE
Lebanon, Pennsylvania

ROGERS, REID REGINALD
Buies Creek, North Carolina
RUMBLEY, JO ANNE
Greensboro, North Carolina
SAMPSON, JUDITH GAIL
Laurel Hill, North Carolina

SANSBURY, AUSTIN BAXTER, JR.
Lumberton, North Carolina
SASSER, KENNETH LINDSEY
Whiteville, North Carolina
SHELLEY, HENRY GRADY, JR
Marion, South Carolina

SHREVE, DAVID PRENTISS
Falls Church, Virginia
SMITH, AGNES ANNE
Grimesland, North Carolina
SMITH, HARRY RANKIN
Greensboro, North Carolina

SMITH, JESSE E.
Mt. Olive, North Carolina
SMITH, PHILIP DEWAR
Fuquay Spring, North Carolina
SNIDER, LLOYD BUTNER
Liberty, North Carolina

SOLES, RICHARD VERNON, JR.
Whiteville, North Carolina
SPELL, ALBERT CHARLES
Hope Mills, North Carolina
SPIVEY, ORIN RALPH, JR.
Roseboro, North Carolina

59

SPIVEY, THOMAS AVERETTE
Roseboro, North Carolina

STANLEY, LARRY MONROE
Clarendon, North Carolina

STARLING, JAMES ALTON, JR.
Pine Level, North Carolina

STEELE, EDOUARD BESSON
Raleigh, North Carolina

STEPHENS, ANNIE LAURA
Fairmont, North Carolina

STEPHENSON, ALTON LOUIS, JR.
Erwin, North Carolina

STRICKLAND, ADDIE JO
Fair Bluff, North Carolina

STRICKLAND, ANNA NEAL
Cerro Gordo, North Carolina

STRICKLAND, JANICE GREY
Clinton, North Carolina

STRICKLAND, WAYNE McCOY
Mt. Olive, North Carolina

SULLIVAN, BRITT EVERETT
Raleigh, North Carolina

TALLEY, KENNETH MATTHEW
Fuquay Springs, North Carolina

19

TAYLOR, JESSIE ALLISON
Wilson, North Carolina

TELFAIR, RICHARD BADGER, JR.
Raleigh, North Carolina

TEMPLE, TOMMY HOYLE
Zebulon, North Carolina

TERRELL, ALVA LEE
Henderson, North Carolina

TERRELL, ANDREW PAGE
Henderson, North Carolina

THOMPSON, GENE ELLIOTT
Elizabethtown, North Carolina

TITMUS, EDWARD BUFORD
Petersburg, Virginia

TRIPP, BETTY JO
Buies Creek, North Carolina

TRIPP, WILLIAM BURTON
Ayden, North Carolina

TURLINGTON, JUNE DARE
Erwin, North Carolina

TURNER, WILLIAM HERBERT
Ahoskie, North Carolina

TWIFORD, LOUIS BRASON
Elizabeth City, North Carolina

WAGNON, BRENDA MAGDELINE
Raleigh, North Carolina
WARD, THOMAS DORSEY
Aynor, South Carolina
WARREN, JANET ROSE
Dunn, North Carolina

WASHER, ROBERT JAMES
Merrick, New York
WEBSTER, FRANCES REBECCA
Madison, North Carolina
WELLS, JAMES WYNN
Roseboro, North Carolina

WELLS, JUANITA INEZ
Harrells, North Carolina
WELLS, NANCY DALLAS
Teachey, North Carolina
WELSH, KENNETH GORDON, JR.
Raleigh, North Carolina

WEST, PERCY WHITE, JR.
Sanford, North Carolina
WHALEY, CAROLE ANNETTE
Kinston, North Carolina
WHELESS, EDITH GRAY
Louisburg, North Carolina

WHITBY, HERMAN WESLEY
Roanoke Rapids, North Carolina
WILLIAMS, BESS JANE
Clayton, North Carolina
WILLIAMS, LOIS ROVINE
Pink Hill, North Carolina

WILLARD, ROBERT WAYNE
Riverside, New Jersey
WILLIAMS, JOHN PEYTON, JR.
Roseboro, North Carolina
WILLIAMS, JUNIUS SNEED
Fayetteville, North Carolina

WILLIAMSON, STEPHEN MONROE
Kenansville, North Carolina
WILSON, DONALD
Bunnlevel, North Carolina
WOOD, JACK FRANKLIN
Martinsville, Virginia

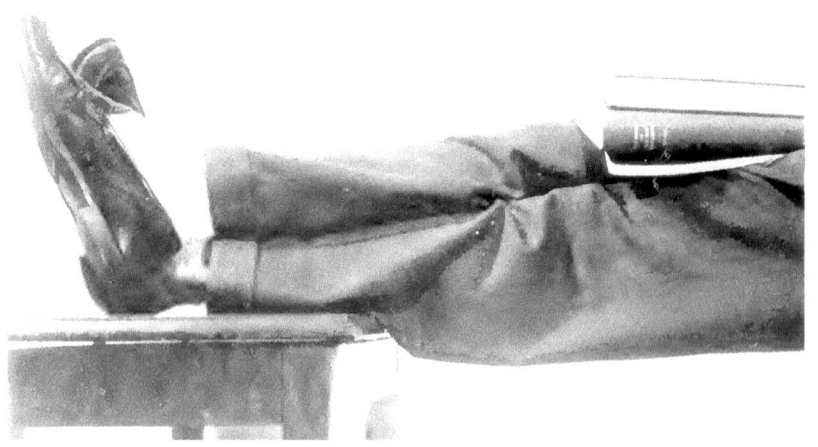

Academy Officers:

BRAXTON MATTHEWS
Vice-President

NANCY HARRIS
Secretary

KEITH NEIGHBORS
President

MISS ORA C. CANSLER
Advisor

Eleventh Grade

First row: BAKER, SIDNEY W., Durham, North Carolina; BURGNER, FOSTER CLINE, Durham, North Carolina; DRAUGHON, DAVID DIXON, Cumberland, North Carolina; DRAWDY, GEORGE ELLIS, Smithfield, North Carolina; HARRIS, NANCY FERN, Norfolk, Virginia; HENWOOD, RICHARD SIDNEY, Elizabeth City, North Carolina. Second row: HOBBS, JUDY BENTON, Aberdeen, North Carolina; KNIGHT, LEE, Fayetteville, North Carolina; MCLAMB, JOE E., Bunnlevel, North Carolina; MOORE, JAMES BALLARD, Cary, North Carolina; REGISTER, JAMES LOUIS, Four Oaks, North Carolina; ROGERS, WILLIAM LUMES, Youngsville, North Carolina. Third row: ROSE, JACK COOPER, Nashville, North Carolina; SMITH, JOHNNIE MAE, Bluffton, South Carolina; STRICKLAND, DELOIT, Dunn, North Carolina; TURNER, ROBERT WILLIAM, Raleigh, North Carolina; WHITE, RAYMOND MARSHALL, Bartow, Florida

Twelfth Grade

Arasta, Houshang
Tehran, Iran

Ashworth, John Wade
Mamers, North Carolina

Byrd, Hazel Lawrence
Myrtle Beach, South Carolina

Collins, Hugh George, Jr.
Fairmont, North Carolina

Corrales, Jaime Pascual
Central Delkias, Oriente, Cuba

Curtis, Jean Audrey
Thomasville, North Carolina

Daughtry, Ludie Jackqueline
Clinton, North Carolina

Dean, Benjamin Franklin
Buies Creek, North Carolina

Elliott, Nancy Arlene
Nichols, South Carolina

Enzor, Laura Anne
Fair Bluff, North Carolina

Estes, Margaret Olivia
Franklinton, North Carolina

Faircloth, Rebecca Dunn
Salemburg, North Carolina

Gove, Linda
Dillon, South Carolina

Gray, Havord R.
Jacksonville, North Carolina

Hall, Stephen Cashwell
New Bern, North Carolina

Harrell, Carlisle Wingate
Norfolk, Virginia

Harrell, Robert Kelly
Norfolk, Virginia

Harrelson, Thomas Joseph
Southport, North Carolina

Hobbs, Nell Brenda
Raleigh, North Carolina

Holleman, Robert Dunn, Jr.
Durham, North Carolina

Homar, Donald Paul
Winchester, Virginia

Hunt, Walter Skelhe
Raleigh, North Carolina

Johnson, Epsie Jo-Ann
Lumberton, North Carolina

Johnson, Henri Pearl
Farmville, North Carolina

Twelfth Grade

King, Durward Elbert, Jr.
Suffolk, Virginia

MacMillan, John Olive
Fayetteville, North Carolina

McGannon, William Edward
Salem, Virginia

Mackey, Thomas Hughes
Lancaster, South Carolina

Matthews, Braxton Ray
Kipling, North Carolina

Moeller, William Paul
Charlotte, North Carolina

Neighbors, Dalma Deith
Benson, North Carolina

Polk, Glenn Eldon, Jr.
Fayetteville, North Carolina

Reddick, Elizabeth Jeanne
Norfolk, Virginia

Rose, Edgar Maurice
Smithfield, North Carolina

Schramm, George
Fort Bragg, North Carolina

Seagroves, Norman Miller
Durham, North Carolina

Small, John Calvin
Buies Creek, North Carolina

Stafford, Charles Lewis
Dunn, North Carolina

Steinberg, David Ronald
Erwin, North Carolina

Stone, Eleanore Ruth
Durham, North Carolina

Thomas, John Mitchell
Bladenboro, North Carolina

Thompson, Margaret Christine
Whiteville, North Carolina

Tuttle, Linda Helen
Norfolk, Virginia

Vaughan, Victoria Elizabeth
Durham, North Carolina

Watson, James Purdie
Moncure, North Carolina

Wayburn, Sam Morris
Raleigh, North Carolina

Weddle, Roberte Lee
Buies Creek, North Carolina

Wiggins, June Gail
Clinton, North Carolina

Wiles, Jim Ravine
N. Wilkesboro, North Carolina

Best, George Robert, Lexington, North Carolina; Cooper, Donald Paul, Durham, North Carolina; Pearce, Clyde Pruitt, Buies Creek, North Carolina; Ragland, Mary Susan, Buies Creek, North Carolina; Stephens, (Mrs.) Edna Sessoms, Erwin, North Carolina.

Special Students

Second Semester Students

First row:
Kamil, Ali, Baghdad, Iraq; Barber, William Richard, Lakeland, Florida; Baughn, Sandra Louise, West End, North Carolina; Best, Tommy Randall, Goldsboro, North Carolina; Boggs, Jean Ann, Dayton, Ohio; Britt, Henry Forest, Fairmont, North Carolina.

Second row:
Brown, Carolyn Beatrice, Lillington, North Carolina; Byrd, David Lincoln, Chadbourn, North Carolina; Carter, Samuel Patrick, Fayetteville, North Carolina; Ehdaie, Houshang, Tehran, Iran; Faircloth, Willie, Goldsboro, North Carolina; Graham, Sylvia Ann, Broadway, North Carolina.

Third row:
Horrell, Mack Raymond, Atkinson, North Carolina; Harrington, Donald Wayne, Moncure, North Carolina; Hobbs, Cecil Wright, Jr., Roseboro, North Carolina; Jennings, Mary Louise, Elizabeth City, North Carolina; Jernigan, Robert Jessie, Newport, North Carolina; Jones, Vernon Walters, Durham, North Carolina.

Second Semester Students

First row:
Kelly, Joseph Harold, Sanford, North Carolina; Kennedy, Vernon Leonard, Kinston, North Carolina; Kirby, James Stanley, Lucama, North Carolina; Lane, Haywood A. Jr., Goldsboro, North Carolina.

Second row:
Lynch, James Mitchell, Jacksonville, North Carolina; Mathis, Alfred Ray, Warsaw, North Carolina; Nelligan, Robert Martin, Lynnhaven, Virginia; Pate, Charles Blue, Rowland, North Carolina; Pate, Donald Quincy, Millbrook, North Carolina; Plummer, Joseph Ted, Fayetteville, North Carolina.

Third row:
Prescott, Jerry Holton, New Bern, North Carolina; Rogers, William, Fuquay Springs, North Carolina; Stephenson, Jackie Hooks, Clayton, North Carolina; Stewart, Kermit Harold, Lillington, North Carolina; Sullivan, Joe Warren, Carthage, North Carolina; Thigpen, John Marvin, Mount Olive, North Carolina.

Fourth row:
Thomas, Johnsie Elizabeth, Charlotte, North Carolina; Todd, James William, Warsaw, North Carolina; Travers, Philip Achillije, Fayetteville, North Carolina; Vanaman, Robert Frederick, Fayetteville, North Carolina; Whitaker, William Jeb, Jr., Youngsville, North Carolina; Williams, Albert Edwin, Smithfield, North, Carolina.

Dr. Leslie Campbell

Dr. Campbell, in this, the silver anniversary year of your presidency, we, the PINE BURR staff, gratefully salute you, and we take the privilege of thanking you for all that you have contributed to our success and well-being.

We are indebted to you for your effective leadership which has placed Campbell College in the front ranks of the junior colleges.

Our experience here has been a turning point for many of us. We have made important decisions concerning our lives and how we shall use them to serve. We are impressed by your unselfish dedication, your Christian example, and your genuine concern for our welfare.

We are resolved to keep alive a warmth in our hearts for our alma mater in appreciation of our pleasant days together.

May the best days for Campbell College lie ever ahead!

Dean A. R. Burkot

Of all the impressions we have gathered here, the memory of you will remain one of the most distinct. For two years, we have seen the endless services you have performed with energetic ease. We have tasted the temperance of your broad-mindedness through our personal acquaintance, and we have shared your vast experience and knowledge through our classroom relationship.

We know from your influence upon and reaction to us that you are vitally interested in us. In response, we wish to acknowledge our own deep and tender gratitude for your faith in us by pledging to fulfill the high hopes you have for us.

We humbly remember you, a fellow Christian devoted to the progress of humanity and the happiness of your home, a man of ceaseless effort and limitless interests, a tower of inspiration.

LONNIE D. SMALL
Business Manager

ROALD H. SORENSON
Director of Public Relations

MRS. EMMA LEIGH HOPSON
Dean of Women

ROBERT L. KING
Registrar
Dean of Men

Faculty

HOWARD EUGENE ALLEN
Psychology
J. NURNEY BOND
Engineering Mathematics
JAMES L. FAISON
Business Education
CHARLES B. HOWARD
Religion

MRS. A. PAUL BAGBY
Latin
MRS. ELIZABETH BRITTON
Chemistry Laboratory
W. CONARD GASS
Social Sciences
B. W. JENKINS
Business Education

HAROLD C. BAIN
Mathematics
MISS ORA C. CANSLER
English
GEORGE S. GRAHAM
Social Sciences
MRS. PHILIP KENNEDY
English

MISS BARBARA BARBER
Speech
GEORGE CLIFTON
Social Sciences
MRS. CHARLES A. HORTON
Music
PHILIP KENNEDY
English

MRS. GRACE BOND
English
DR. MARTHA E. EDWARDS
Mathematics
CHARLES A. HORTON
Music
DR. PERRY Q. LANGSTON
Religious Education

Faculty

Top row:
MRS. CARL LLOYD
Physical Education
DAVID LOCKWOOD
Art
MRS. A. E. LYNCH
Music
FRED McCALL
Biology, Physical Education
MISS CHARLOTTE MIX
Spanish
E. L. NELSON
Physics, Biology

Second row:
ROBERT LEE NEWTON
Religion
DONALD E. PHELPS
Modern Language
HERMAN PHELPS
Business Education
MISS GERALDINE PERKINS
Music
MISS MABEL POWELL
English
MISS NELL POWELL
Mathematics

Third row:
MRS. G. T. PROFFIT
Chemistry
THOMAS CROFT RUTHERFORD
Biology, Chemistry
MRS. INEZ G. SADLER
Business Education
MRS. GEORGE SWANN
English
DR. JOHN THOMPSON
Mathematics
G. A. TRIPP
Social Sciences

Fourth row:
MRS. WILLIAM P. TUCK
Home Economics
WILLIAM PRESSLEY TUCK
Social Sciences
ALAN TUTTLE
Mathematics
E. M. WALKER
Biology
MISS MARY JANE WHITE
English

Staff

DR. BRUCE BLACKMON
College Physician

MRS. H. B. DAVIS
College Nurse

MRS. CECELIA GODWIN
Secretary to Business Manager

MRS. A. R. BURKOT
Laundry Manager

H. B. DAVIS
Assistant Director of Athletics

MRS. KYLE GREGORY
Secretary to Superintendent of Buildings and Grounds

REV. WELDON JOHNSON
College Pastor

F. M. CAUDELL
Bookstore Manager

MRS. ETHEL EUBANKS
Assistant to Dean of Women

MISS JESSIE CLEGG GRIFFIN
Librarian

ALLEN JONES
Assistant to Superintendent of Buildings and Grounds

TOM COLLINS
Director of Student Activities

MRS. JAMES L. FAISON
Secretary to Dean

MRS. JACKIE HOLT
Assistant Secretary to Business Manager

MRS. EUGENE LASATER
Alumni Secretary

MRS. CARL DAVIS
Bookkeeper

MRS. TOM GILBERT
Assistant to Dean of Women

MRS. B. W. JENKINS
Dietitian

Staff

Mrs. Lucy Lasater	Mrs. M. B. Matthews, Jr.	Mrs. Robert H. Morgan	Mrs. Jack Ragland	Miss Mary Susan Ragland
Secretary to Public Relations Director	*Secretary to President*	*Cashier*	*Assistant Librarian*	*Secretary in Public Relations*
Mrs. Dewey Rogers	Mrs. Edna Stephens	Ashley Stewart	Mrs. Hazel Stewart	Mrs. Ray Hall
Bookstore Clerk	*Secretary to Registrar*	*Superintendent of Buildings and Grounds*	*Assistant Dietitian*	*Transcript Clerk*

John E. Ayscue
Professor Emeritus

Miss Ada Overby
Assistant to the Dean Retired

B. P. Marshbanks, Sr.
Business Manager, Emeritus

Alumni Executive Committee

A. HARTWELL CAMPBELL
President
Greenville, North Carolina

NORMAN A. WIGGINS
Vice-President
Winston-Salem, North Carolina

MRS. E. H. LASATER
Secretary and Treasurer
Buies Creek, North Carolina

JACK KITCHIN
Norfolk, Virginia

MRS. MAC SATTERWHITE
Oxford, North Carolina

Alumni Council

MRS. HELEN CARR BIGHAM
Charlotte, North Carolina

DR. BRUCE BLACKMON
Buies Creek, North Carolina

REV. J. BOYCE BROOKS
Greensboro, North Carolina

DR. VICTOR BROWN
Williamston, North Carolina

C. A. DANDELAKE
Four Oaks, North Carolina

DOUGLAS DEAN
Clayton, North Carolina

JOE EASOM
Butner, North Carolina

ROBERT HARRIS
Spray, North Carolina

DR. LEOPOLD M. HAYS
High Point, North Carolina

GLEN JERNIGAN
Fayetteville, North Carolina

BERLES JOHNSON
Lillington, North Carolina

MISS GERRY MATTHEWS
Erwin, North Carolina

REV. JOHN B. MCCRIMMON
Bladenboro, North Carolina

MRS. T. BRAGG MCLEOD
Charlotte, North Carolina

J. EVERETTE MILLER
Raleigh, North Carolina

H. P. NAYLOR
Roseboro, North Carolina

MRS. MAC SATTERWHITE
Oxford, North Carolina

MRS. LEROY TOWNSEND
Lumberton, North Carolina

Trustees

Rev. Herbert W. Baucom, Jr.	Oxford, N. C.	Rev. Ben C. Fisher	Wake Forest, N. C.
Dr. Claud B. Bowen	Greensboro, N. C.	John C. Fletcher, Jr.	Charlotte, N. C.
H. Spurgeon Boyce	Durham, N. C.	Roscoe Griffin	Rocky Mount, N. C.
Dr. J. Street Brewer	Roseboro, N. C.	Rev. Maurice Grissom	Elizabeth City, N. C.
W. Carroll Bryan	Jacksonville, N. C.	M. S. Hayworth	Rocky Mount, N. C.
R. D. Bine	Fayetteville, N. C.	Blanton A. Hartness	Henderson, N. C.
Rev. Roy Clifford	Lexington, N. C.	R. A. Hedgepeth	Lumberton, N. C.
Rev. Howard G. Dawkins	Kinston, N. C.	Rev. Dennis Hockaday	Durham, N. C.

Trustees

I. B. Julian	Fayetteville, N. C.	Rev. Ernest P. Russell	Dunn, N. C.
Fred R. Keith	Lumberton, N. C.	Mrs. J. H. Strickland	Four Oaks, N. C.
Willis E. Kivett	Southern Pines, N. C.	Dr. Charles R. Tucker	Parkton, N. C.
Charles W. McEnally	New Bern, N. C.	Earl McD. Westbrook	Dunn, N. C.
Mrs. W. E. Nichols	Coats, N. C.	F. Carter Williams	Raleigh, N. C.
Charles S. Norwood	Goldsboro, N. C.	Mrs. Robert W. Winston	Lillington, N. C.
Roy M. Purser	Raleigh, N. C.	W. M. Womble	Sanford, N. C.
Mrs. W. K. Rand	Durham, N. C.	Carl Worley, Sr.	Selma, N. C.

Board of Trustees

Epsilon Pi Eta

Delores Kube
Sylvia Grubbs
Raleigh Castelloe
Elmund Hughes
Rita McLean

PURPOSE

Epsilon Pi Eta, honor society, was organized for the purpose of promoting character, leadership, and scholarship. Requirements for membership are the attaining of a fixed scholarship record for at least one year and the nomination of at least twenty-five per cent of both the faculty and members of the society.

Student Council

ADVISORS
Mrs. Thelma Gilbert
Mrs. Emma Lee Hopson
Mrs. Ethel Eubanks
A. R. Burkot
Robert L. King

OFFICERS
Delores Kube
Secretary
Gordon Fearing
President
Raleigh Castelloe
Vice-President

PURPOSE

The purpose of this organization is to foster a better relationship and understanding between all groups that are connected in any way with Campbell College and to promote good citizenship and a genuine school loyalty by precept and example.

Seated: Herman Phelps, Faculty Advisor; Delores Kube, Gordon Fearing, Raleigh Castelloe, Harold Bain, Faculty Advisor. *Standing:* Mary Lee Chilton, Caroline Padgette, Dan Spalding, R. C. Norris, Saundra Bryan, Gordon Clark, Benny Hocutt, Shirley Minton, Keith Neighbors, Arthur Cobb.

Women's Executive Council

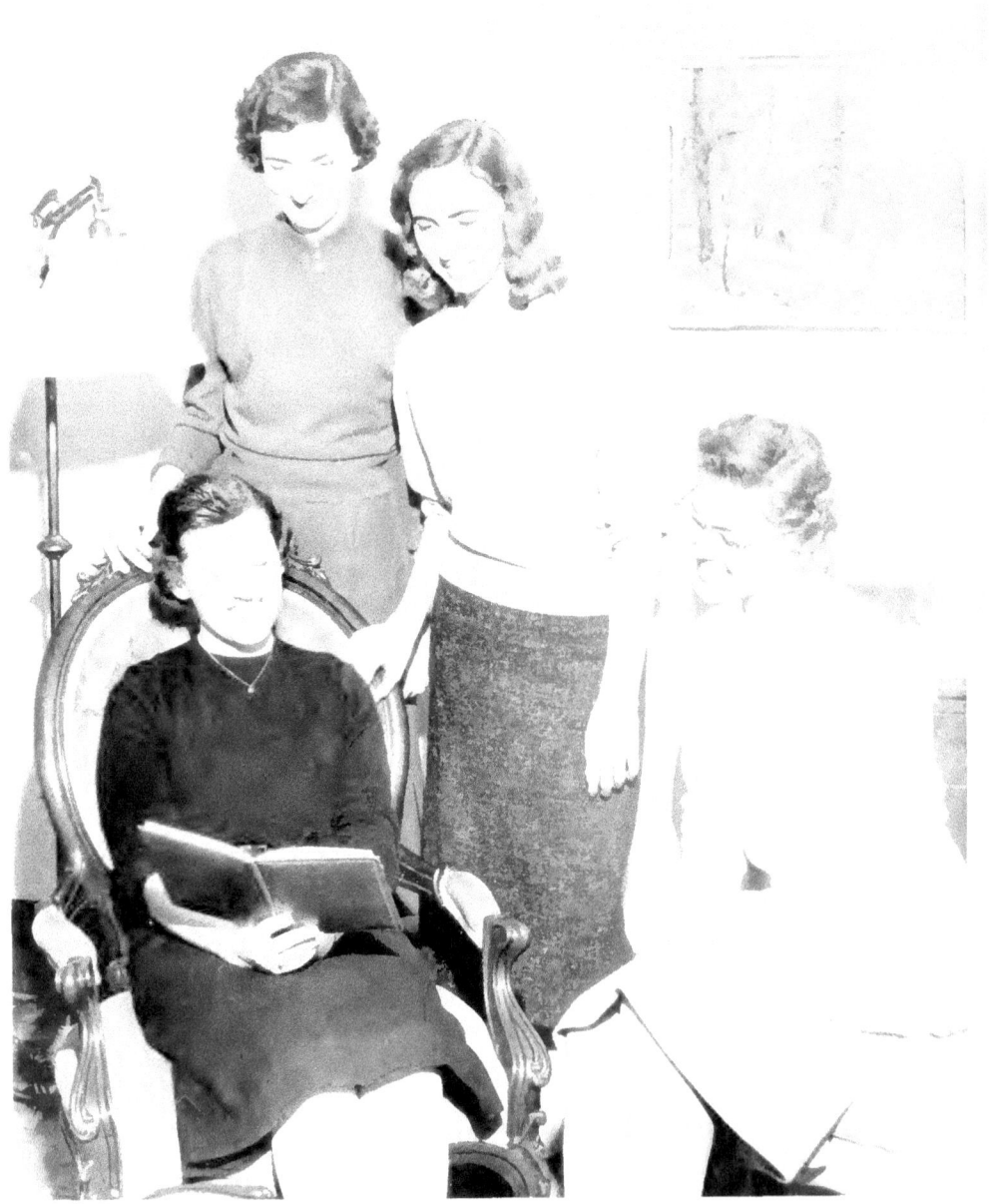

GERRY DEWBERRY
Executive President

FRANCES LEONARD
Treat Dorm President

SYLVIA GRUBBS
New Dorm President

ANNE RUMBLEY
Day Dorm President

Dormitory Hostesses

Mrs. Thelma Gilbert
Treat

Mrs. Emma Lee Hopson
Day

Mrs. Ethel Eubanks
New

Day House Council

Anne Rumbley
Annie Jo Griffin
Maxine Elliott
Mary Lee Chilton
Janice Vest
Betty Rose Wilson
Ann Phillips

NEW HOUSE COUNCIL

Sylvia Grubbs, Jesse Taylor, Gerry Dewberry, Daphne Snell, Irene Blake, Billie Dunn, Nancy Wells, Sarah Klugel, Anita Neal Strickland, Katherine Almy, Billie Creech

TREAT HOUSE COUNCIL

Erma Williams, Jan Ammons, Linda Barcus, Edith Wrekas, Betsy Barefoot, Frances

TONY FASTIGE
Pearson Dorm President

ROBERT L. KING
Advisor

ALEX BRYAN
Axxxx President

ROBERT BERRY
Pxxxxx House Pxxxxxxx

Men's Executive Council

JOHNNY GAINES
Layton Dorm President

ARTHUR COBB
Executive President

TOM ROSE
Kitchen Dorm President

BOB RICHARDS
Farm House President

RALPH SPxxEY
Britt Dorm President

MEN'S DORMITORY HOSTS

Tom Collins
Britt

Harold Bain
Kitchen

H. B. Davis
Layton and Annex

FARM HOUSE COUNCIL

Bob Richards

Tommy Eddins

Vernon Crumpler

BRITT HOUSE COUNCIL
Tom Collins, *Advisor*; Ralph Spivey, Frank Mayo, Nelson Reuschling, Ronald Cunningham, Dayton Capps.

KITCHEN HOUSE COUNCIL
Steve Williams, Tom Rose, David Day, Billy Buffaloe, Donald Cooper, Gordon Harrison, Gene Carr.

ANNEX HOUSE COUNCIL

Alex Bryan

Doug Simpson

PARKER HOUSE COUNCIL

Robert Berry

Bob Moore

Jim Trader

LAYTON DORM COUNCIL
Johnny Gaines, Tom Ward, Bill Dewberry, Kenneth Sodergren, Walt Moore

PEARSON DORM COUNCIL
Wilbur Hargrove, Tony Fastige, Lawrence Gaskins, Elwood Bass

Baptist Student Union

EXECUTIVE COUNCIL

Robert Adams	President
Delores Kube	Vice-President
Judy Sampson	Devotional Chairman
Patsy Hughes	Social Chairman
Charles Rigsbee	Enlistment Chairman
Betty Ann Britt	Secretary
Barbara McLamb	Publicity Chairman
Gordon Harrison	Vesper Co-Chairman
Gerry Dewberry	Vesper Co-Chairman
Betty Jo Tripp	Stewardship Chairman
David McGugan	Ministerial Association Representative
Sylvia Grubbs	Music Chairman
Raleigh Castelloe	Sunday School Representative
Annie Jo Griffin	B.T.U. Representative
Bill Dewberry	Brotherhood Representative
Daphne Snell	Listen Offering Chairman
Billie Dunn	Y.W.A. Representative

PURPOSE

The Baptist Student Union strives to promote spiritual and moral growth of the individual student through a campus program. The objectives of this program are to develop balanced Christian personalities and remove all roadblocks to a deeper spiritual and intellectual affirmation of faith and to promote stewardship and missions.

B. S. U.

MISS ORA CANSLER
B. S. U. Advisor

TOM COLLINS
B. S. U. Director

ROALD SORENSON
B. T. U. Director

J. NURNEY BONO
Sunday School Superintendent

GREATER COUNCIL

Seated: Betty Barnes, Carolyn Brown, Mary Bullard, Ronald Cunningham, Betty Lou Ellen, Robert Parnell, Benny Hocutt. *Standing:* Barbara Stewart, J. D. Gore, Sue Taylor, Nancy Miller, Jennie Faye Minnis, Becky Webster, Evelyn Cook, Ione Jones, Betty Ann Harrell, George Hayes, Jimmy Young.

Ministerial Conference

First row: Waverly Atkins, Ronald Baird, John Bland, Kennard Brackney, David Brooks, Raleigh Castelloe, William Caudle, Ronald Clapp, Charles Coats. Second row: Bill Denton, Bill Dewberry, Gerry Dewberry, Billie Dunn, Marvin Gaster, A B Green, Betty Ann Harrell, Bill Hawkins, George Hayes. Third row: Ralph Holt, Betty Ruth Jones, Courtney Kennemur, Delores Kube, Billy Lee, Margaret Lennon, Frances Leonard, Elizabeth McCraw, David McGugan. Fourth row: Jim Murphy, Wayne Oakley, James Olive, Robert Parnell, Clyde Pearce, Nelson Reuschling, Jack Rose, Anne Rumbley, Willie Shepard. Fifth row: Dan Spalding, Howard Stokes, Daphne Stubbs, Vernon Sullivan, James Trader, Thomas Ward, Herman Whitby, Sonja Williford, Benny Wood. Sixth row: Jimmie Young, Tommy Young, Ernest M Walker, Charles B Howard.

OFFICERS

President   BILL HAWKINS

Vice-President   RALPH HOLT

Secretary
     BETTY ANN HARRELL

Treasurer   GERRY DEWBERRY

PURPOSE

The Ministerial Conference Class meets weekly affording students the opportunity of hearing well-trained speakers from churches and church-related institutions. Sophomore ministerial students prepare and deliver sermons to the Conference during the spring semester.

This class offers to young men and women training and experience necessary for Christian service.

Religious Education Club

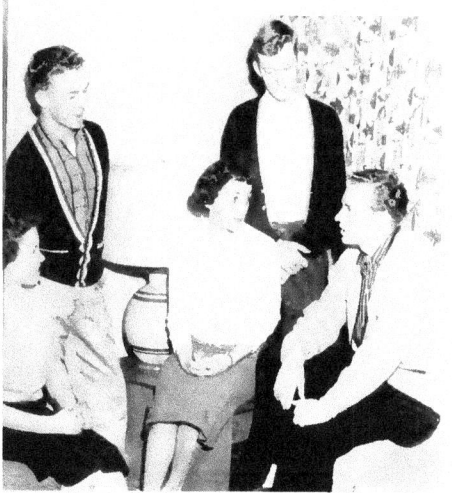

OFFICERS

EDITH WHELESS	Social Chairman
JIMMY YOUNG	Program Chairman
SONJA WILLIFORD	Secretary-Treasurer
JIM McCALL	Vice-President
BILL DEWBERRY	President

DR. AND MRS. PERRY Q. LANGSTON
Sponsors of Religious Education Club

PURPOSE

The Religious Education Club strives to promote interest and enthusiasm among the students in Christian education. This organization is open to all members of the student body.

First row: Betty Ann Harrell, Bill Dewberry, Mary Lee Chilton, Gerry Dewberry, Jimmy Young, Jennie Faye Minnis, Benny Hocutt. *Second row:* Judy Sampson, Edith Wheless, Bill Hawkins, Anne Rumbley, Sue Taylor, Becky Webster, Mary Bullard, Wayne Oakley. *Third row:* Scarlet Hill, Evelyn Eakes, Sonja Williford, Linda Holt, Delores Kube, George Hayes, Jean Creede, David McGugan, Evelyn Cook. *Fourth row:* Phil Travers, Billie Dunn, Ronald Baird, Frances Leonard, Jim McCall, Willie Shepherd, Betty Ruth Jones, Waverly Atkins.

Young Women's Auxiliary

Seated: Linda Tuttle, Mary Zillah Bennett, Dencie Brown, Jean Creede, Barbara Stewart, Jennie Faye Minnis, Delores Kube, Nancy Gentry, Betty Lou Ellen, Sonja Williford. Standing: Billie Dunn, Betty Ruth Jones, Mary Bullard, Beverly White, Frances Leonard, Mary Lee Chilton, Anne Rumbley, Sue Taylor, Betty Ann Harrell, Gerry Dewberry.

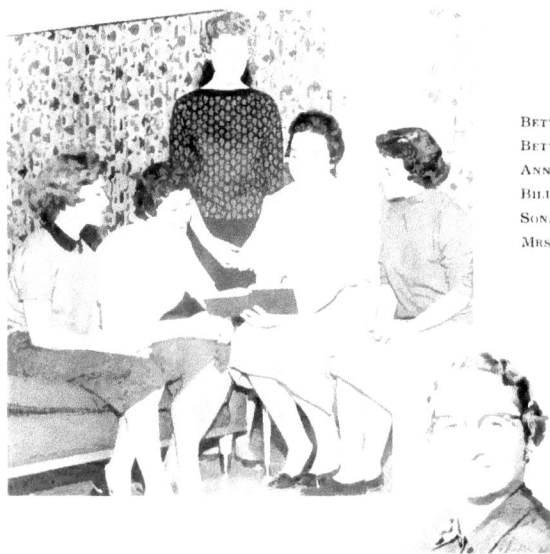

OFFICERS

Betty Lou Ellen	Vice-President
Betty Ruth Jones	Social Chairman
Anne Rumbley	Program Chairman
Billie Dunn	President
Sonja Williford	Secretary-Treasurer
Mrs. Perry Q. Langston	Counselor

PURPOSE

The Young Women's Auxiliary teaches young women about missions and the world's needs. The members of this organization set out to help in meeting these needs.

Arthur Cobb, Caroline Padgette, Linda Gove, Betsy Barefoot, Eugene Carter, Nelson Reuschling, Braxton Matthews, Marvin Bishop, John Thomas, Bill Butler, Charles Lashley.

Methodist Student Movement

PURPOSE

Organized this fall, the Methodist Student Movement has among its purposes the improvement of each student's ability to better himself and his campus. It intends to group the Methodist students together both religiously and socially.

Robert L. Newton
Advisor

Canterbury Club

Front row: Jack Colley, Jim Trader, Conrad Bailey, Thomas C. Rutherford. *Back row:* Gordon Fearing, Richard Henwood, Bill McIver.

PURPOSE

The Canterbury Club was newly organized this year to provide an opportunity for Episcopal young people to join in fellowship and worship and proclaim the Lordship of Christ to all men.

This organization trains young people for the lay ministry and helps them in obtaining their Lay Readers License.

THOMAS C. RUTHERFORD
Sponsor

Collegiate Council for the United Nations

OFFICERS

NELSON REUSCHLING
President

TOMMY CLEMMONS
Vice-President

MARY LEE CHILTON
Secretary-Treasurer

PURPOSE

The Collegiate Council for the United Nations is composed of students interested in international affairs and, in particular, the activities of the United Nations. The organization is composed of many chapters located on campuses in the United States and Canada. Nelson Reuschling, president, was chosen last year to attend the Thirteenth Annual Intercollegiate United Nations Seminar in New York City.

Seated: Billy Buffaloe, Mary Lee Chilton, Nelson Reuschling, Mr. Donald Phelps, Advisor; Tommy Clemmons, Anne Rumbley. *Standing*: Jack Colley, Marvin Bishop, Ralph Spivey, Katie Lou Hannon, David Brooks, Charles James, Gordon Fearing, Brenda Wagnon.

Music

Touring Choir

Charles Horton, *Director*

CHOIR OFFICERS

Bill Dewberry	*President*
Daphne Snell	*Librarian*
Betsy Carroll	*Social Chairman*
Gordon Clark	*Publicity Chairman*
Braxton Matthews	*Tour Manager*

Department

Mozart Music Club

Braxton Matthews
Sylvia Grubbs
Bob Washer
Jean Creed
Barbara Stewart
Judy Cameron
Curtis Ballard
Margaret Merritt
Bill Campbell
Betty Lou Ellen
Buddy Burton
Daphne Stubbs
Rebecca Stephens
Evelyn Eakes
Henri Pearl Johnson
Courtney Kennemur
Dencie Brown
David Shreve
Bella Mae Stewart

OFFICERS

DAVID SHREVE
President

SYLVIA GRUBBS
Secretary

Community Concert Series

Miss Eleanor Knapp, well-known opera singer of New York and Europe, was guest artist when the opera workshop presented Gian-Carlo Menotti's "The Medium." Campbell student William Autry played the role of Toby.

Walter Carringer, New York concert singer and soloist with the Robert Shaw Chorale was guest soloist with the Campbell College choir during its spring tour.

The "Little Gaelic Singers" is a troupe of Irish singers and dancers who presented a concert delightful to look at and listen to at Campbell College in March. They recently made two appearances on the Ed Sullivan show.

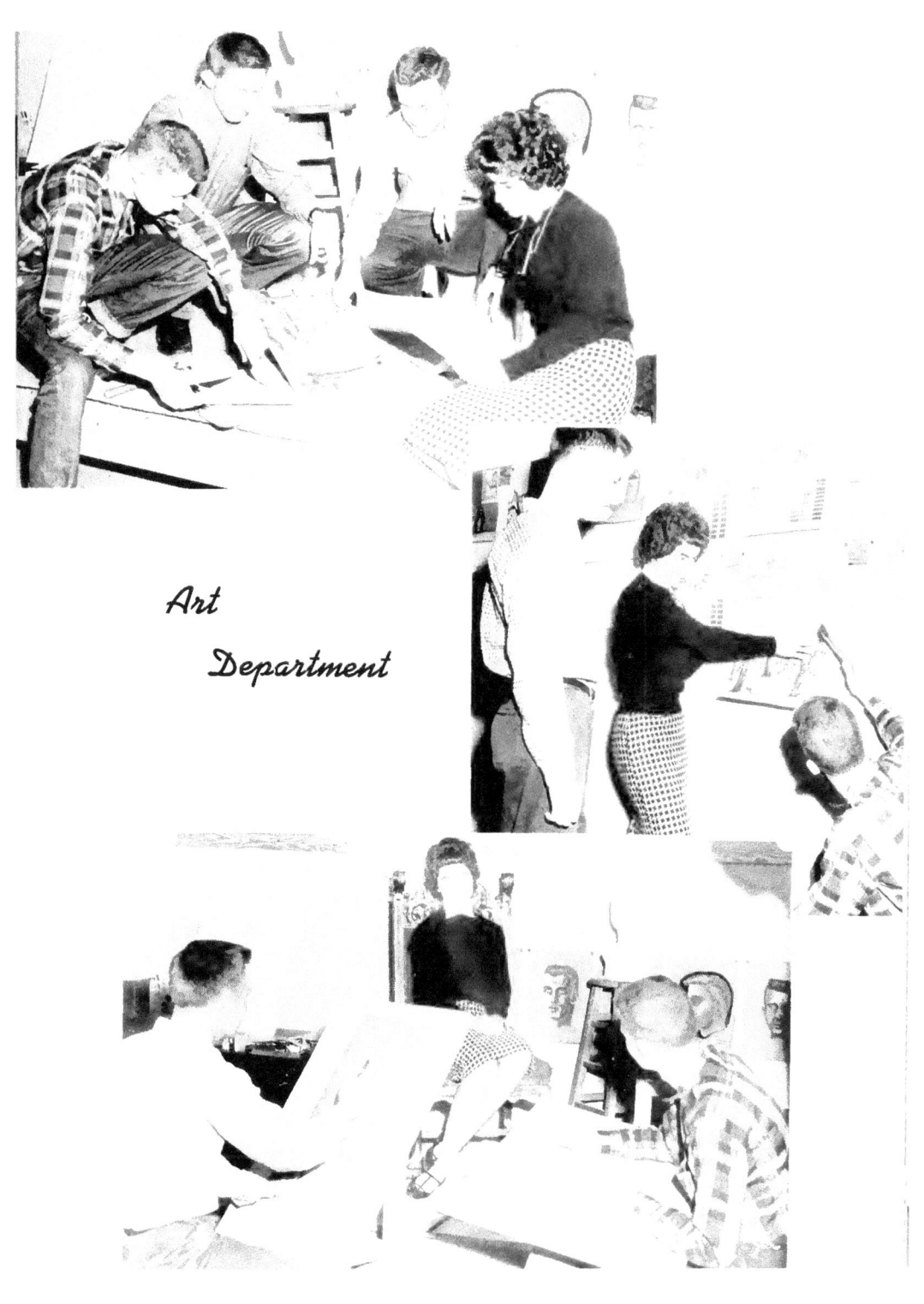

Art Department

Alpha Beta Gamma

First row: Joyce Clark, Rita McLean, Ruth Stone, Theodosia Stewart, Annie Jo Griffin, Lynn Jackson, Morton Fleishman. *Second row:* Charles Henry James, Sue Williams, Carol Roberts, Freed Nackley, Charles Lashley, Mrs. Britton, Gordon Harrison. *Third row:* Marion Creech, David McLeod, Lanny Howell, Edward Titmus, Larry Avery, Mrs. Gilbert, Mrs. Proffit. *Fourth row:* Richard Coughenour, Deward Sykes, Joe Harden, Sam Walker. *Fifth row:* Thomas Hepler, Richard Henwood, Robert Collie, Frank Mayo.

OFFICERS

Morton Fleishman	President
Rita McLean	Secretary
Tom Rose	Treasurer
Nelson Reuschling	Parliamentarian

ADVISORS

Mrs. G. T. Proffit
Mrs. George Britton

PURPOSE

Alpha Beta Gamma is an honorary and social chemistry fraternity organized to promote interest in the field of chemistry and to create fellowship among students of chemistry. Each member must have met the requirements of scholarship and conducted an experiment or presented an original paper before the initiatory assembly. The Chemistry fraternity of Campbell College is the Zeta Chapter.

Future Business Leaders of America

OFFICERS

Seated: Jo Ann McLeod, Secretary; Tommy Clemmons, President. *Standing:* Don Angell, Parliamentarian; Sally Bunn, Treasurer; Stacy Lamm, Vice-President.

PURPOSE

The FBLA strives to promote high ideals and good business practices among its members as well as provide opportunity for practical experience.

First row, left to right: Mrs. Inez Sadler, Sponsor; Wanda Brown, Sally Bunn, Tommy Clemmons, Stacy Lamm, Jo Ann McLeod, Don Angell. *Second row:* Carolyn Hill, Jean Creede, Irene Blake, Betty Rose Wilson, Linda Lee, Bettie Barnes, Gayle Swain, Eunice Hood, Daphne Snell. *Third row:* Judith Maharg, Bill McIver, Eugenia Wilkinson, Murphy Rivenbark, Bettie Ruth Jones.

First row: Louis Woodard, Glen Jernigan, Sonja Williford, Rebecca Lynch, Janet Harrington, Mrs. A. Paul Bagby, Advisor. Second row: Harold Ausley, David Brooks, Juanita Wells, Olivia Estes. Third row: Bill Denton, Braxton Matthews, Jim Trader, Bobby Rowe, Willie Shepard, Vernon Sullivan.

Sodalitas Latina

OFFICERS

GLEN JERNIGAN	President
BOBBY ROWE	Vice-President

PURPOSE

Sodalitas Latina is open to all students who are taking Latin. Its purpose is to acquaint members with Roman life and ideas and to make use of the language through games, songs, and contests.

Spanish Club

OFFICERS

Jean Bond	Secretary
Bill McIver	Vice-President
Bill Hawkins	President

PURPOSE

Campbell College Spanish Club was organized September 1956; and has a two-fold purpose: First, to promote an interest in Spanish culture. Second, for the amusement of students who are studying the language. Through its activities we hope to relieve the pressure of classroom study.

First row: Conrad Bailey, Bill McIver, Bill Hawkins, Miss Charlotte Mix, Advisor; Jean Bond, Jimmy Young. *Second row:* Ronald Cunningham, Linda Rogers, Beverly White, Bill Dewberry, Howard Stokes. *Third row:* George Lancaster, Deward Sykes, Jaime Corrales, Rafael Hernandez, Bill McGannon. *Fourth row:* Arthur Cobb, Harold Little, Mary Bullard, Marie Lewis, Linda Tuttle, Bill Moore, Gene Anderson, Hubert Grimmer, James Butts, Woodrow Briggs.

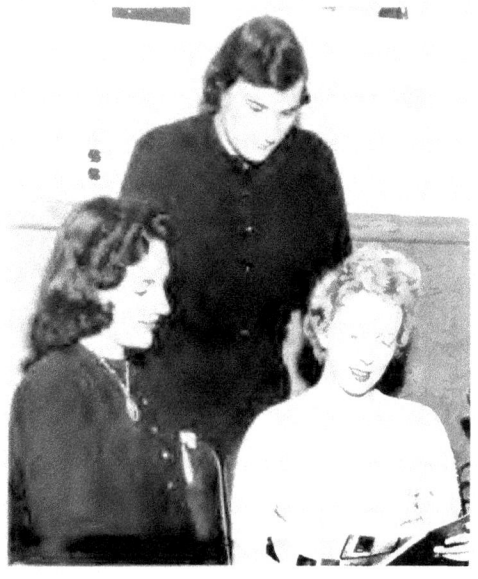

Eta Pi

OFFICERS

BARBARA STEWART	President
MARGARET MONTAGUE	Treasurer
BESS WILLIAMS	Secretary

PURPOSE

The purpose of Eta Pi is to prepare young women of today to become better homemakers of tomorrow.

Seated: Mrs. W. P. Tuck, Advisor; Joyce Clark, Carolyn Wilson, Sara Frances Wilson, Bess Williams, Mary Bennett. *Standing:* Lib Easterling, Shirley Minton, Kitty Lewis, Barbara Stewart, Billie Creech, Margaret Montague.

Debating Club

Tommy Clemmons, Caroline Padgette, David McGugan, Freed Nackley, Mickey Dawson, Howard Stokes, Don Angel, Waverly Atkins.

WILLIAM P. TUCK
Advisor

PURPOSE

Organized last fall, the Debating Club has among its purposes the improvement of each member's ability to uncover information on leading problems of the day, to evaluate that information, and to present it persuasively in a formal debate.

Kitchen Club

Seated, left to right: Linda Davis, Anna Neal Strickland, Betty Jo Tripp, Delores Kube, Marie Lewis, Betty Ann Harrell, Eunice Hood, Peggy Williford, Ronny Ellis, Barbara Griffin, Carolyn Brown, Edith Wheless, Sonja Williford, Daphne Stubbs. Standing, left to right: Louis Woodard, Thomas Hepler, Turner Rivenbark, Bobby Parnell, Ronald Clapp, Waverly Atkins, George Hayes, Mrs. Hazel Stewart.

The Kitchen Club is made up of students who work in the dining hall part-time. They help you, they serve you, they feed you.

The "Creek Pebbles" Staff

Standing: Stevie Starling, Brenda Wagnon, Thomas Hepler, Joan McLeod, Larry Crawford, Jean Bond, Marvin Bishop, Mary Zilah Bennett, Sue Williams, Peggy Williford, and Billy Buffaloe. *Seated:* Pat Carter, Rita McLean, Gordon Clark, and Mr. Philip Kennedy.

Creek Pebbles, the school paper, founded in 1925, is published twice monthly during the school year. This is the official organ of the student body of Campbell College.

Member of the Associated Collegiate Press

GORDON CLARK
Editor

ASSOCIATE EDITORS

Rita McLean

Jean Bond

Brenda Wagnon

Pat Carter

MR. PHILIP C. KENNEDY
Advisor

THE *Pine*

MARY LEE CHILTON
Editor

BARBARA MCLAMB
Feature Editor

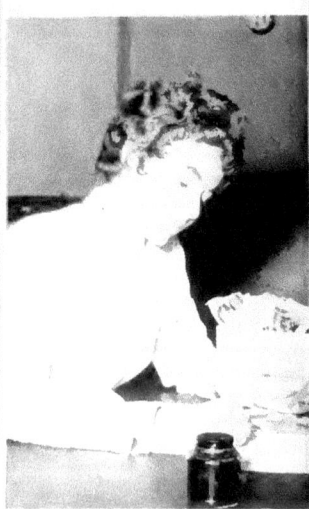
OLIVIA ESTES
Art Editor

BILLY BUFFALOE
Photographer

VICTOR GARRARD
Assistant Business Manager

NELSON REUSCHLING
Business Manager

STAFF

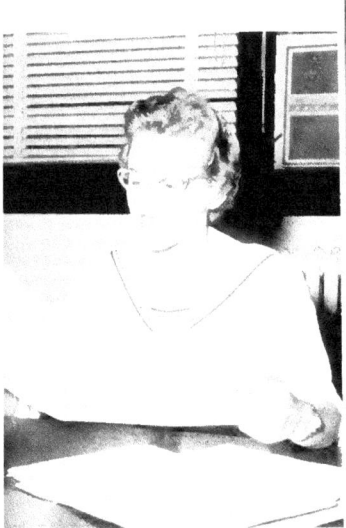

Anne Rumbley
Copy Editor

Jo Ann McLeod
Assistant Copy Editor

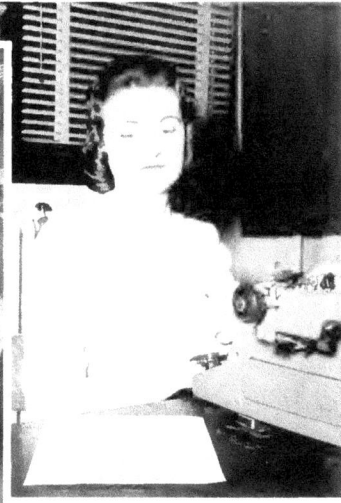

Wanda Brown
Assistant Copy Editor

Rita McLean
Sports Editor

Gordon Welsh
Sports Editor

Mr. Robert L. King
Advisor

This Was Your Life

The links of a charm bracelet hold together a motley array of symbols representing many varied interests. Considered apart, each of these presents its distinctiveness and bids for its share of attention. Encircling the wrist or arm, the ornament carries an impression of unity and enhances the attractiveness of the wearer.

Not unlike a charm bracelet, the PINE BURR is a virtual kaleidoscope of days falling like autumn leaves from the academic calendar caught in a whirl of excitement. Glimpses of individuals and groups recapture only in part the memory of events and activities which engaged the attention of Campbell students during the past months.

Inevitably, there is a degree of sameness from year to year and from college to college. Also, the pattern and rhythm of extra-curricular interests remain fairly constant. What makes for the particular appeal of this year's record is the fact that you were there.

Participant or spectator, relive the headlines made by our athletic teams or re-enact the role of lesser prominence of intramural competition. Performer or listener, review the hours of preparation that went into your enjoyment of the programs of choir or club. Leader or follower, share again the deep concern for our personal welfare evidenced by religious and student government groups. Writer or reader, thrill at the satisfaction of seeing your name or picture in print. Queen or candidate, officer or nominee, recall the anxiety of awaiting the outcome of an election. This was your life!

HOMECOMING

Queen
JANICE VEST

Queen's Court

Tournament Queen

BETTY BARNES

Harvest Festival

JEWEL BLOWE
Queen

BENNY HOCUTT
King

MAY KING

Herbert Turner

MAY QUEEN

Ann Raynor

HONOR ATTENDANTS

Becky Webster, MAID OF HONOR
Harry Smith, KING'S ATTENDANT

ROBERT ADAMS

WANDA BROWN

JEWEL BLOWE

GORDON FEARING

GLENN JERNIGAN

DENCIE BROWN

GORDON CLARK

LINDA BARNES

BARBARA STEWART

JEFF ADAMS

SCARLETT HILL

GENE CARTER

BOB BEST

JANICE VEST

TOMMY HARRELSON

OLIVIA ESTES

OUTSTANDING STUDENTS

DELORES KUBE

BILLY BUFFALOE

ANNE RUMBLEY

GORDON FEARING

GERRY DEWBERRY

BILL DEWBERRY

DOROTHY COLEMAN
Best All Around
Salutatorian

MARGARET CARTER
Runner-Up Best All Around

RUDOLPH LAMONE
College Valedictorian

MARK PRINCE
Athletic Award

WANDA BROWN
Athletic Award

JOYCE STONE
Business Valedictorian

June 1958
Commencement Honors

WANDA ADAMS
High School Valedictorian

BLANCHE RAYNOR
Citizenship

EMMANUEL PEGRAM
Wake Forest Scholarship

KATHRYN ROWLAND
Meredith Scholarship

NANCY SHEARIN
Meredith Scholarship

HUGH McDONALD
Mathematics Achievement Award

GRADUATION 1958

Sports

Head Coach
FRED McCALL

ROBERT ADAMS
Co-Captain

SONNY BAKER
Co-Captain

Assistant Coach
HARGROVE DAVIS

Front row, left to right: Glenwood Byrd, Manager, Perry Holland, Gerald Quick, Ronnie Atkinson, Jeff Adams, Sonny Baker
Second row, left to right: Jimmy Vaughn, Jerry Highsmith, Robert Adams, John Josephson, Jackie Reinhardt, Adolph Hinson, Jim Wiles

 Robert Adams
 Sonny Baker
 Ronnie Atkinson
 Gerald Quick

 Jim Wiles
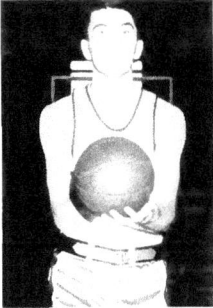 John Josephson
 Jackie Reinhardt
 Jerry Highsmith

 Perry Holland
 Jeff Adams
 Adolph Hinson
 Jimmy Vaughn

Hey, Robert—how do you like my new Calypso suit?

Excellent! Now get in there and fight!

What's this thing, Jim?

Forget the score — what's your name, honey?

What's the score, Jim?

Coach McCall (center) talks with his four sophomore stars about the up coming game. *Left to right:* Gerald Quick, Sonny Baker, Coach, Robert Adams and Ronnie Atkinson.

HIGHLIGHTS

The debut of the '58-'59 edition of Coach Fred McCall's five was made against the strong and talented McCrary Eagles, a team made up of past college stars. Campbell lost but not without giving the Eagles a hard time before they won 98 to 83. Co-Captain Sonny Baker, Ronnie Atkinson, Co-Captain Robert Adams and Gerald Quick all hit in the double figures and looked like the season veterans that McCall was looking for. The four of them are the only returnees from last year's state championship team. Jim Wiles, a newcomer, was very impressive for Campbell hitting for 16 points.

CAMPBELL 78—LOUISBURG 67

In a non-conference game played at Smithfield, Campbell beat Louisburg in a closely fought game. Gerald Quick, Sonny Baker and Jim Wiles were the leading scorers getting 16, 15, and 14 points, respectively.

CAMPBELL 70—E. M. I. 79

Campbell had four players who hit in the double figures but was still unable to grab a victory from E. M. I. It was the first conference game for both teams. Gerald Quick, Sonny Baker, and newcomer John Josephson ripped the nets for 13 points each.

CAMPBELL 65—WINGATE 68

After leading by a point at half-time, Campbell was unable to get rolling in the second half and came out on the short end of the final score. Sonny Baker and Ronnie Atkinson hit for 17 and 14 points. Big Robert Adams pulled down 11 rebounds and pushed in 13 points.

CAMPBELL 93—CHARLOTTE 36

Blasting Charlotte right off the court by a 93 to 36 score, Campbell won its first conference game. Every player on the team scored, with Jackie Reinhardt and Jimmy Vaughn's getting 13 points each; Sonny Baker, Perry Holland and Jeff Adams tallied 10 each.

CAMPBELL 78—FREDRICK 67

McCall's boys won their second straight conference game by beating Fredrick 78 to 67. Sonny Baker was high scorer with 15 points.

CAMPBELL 77—P. J. C. 73

After a hard fight to the finish, Campbell was able to come out on top over P. J. C. Ronnie Atkinson was the big man for the Camels, getting 17 points; Gerald Quick was close behind with 15.

CAMPBELL 70—U. N. C. FRESHMEN 79

Campbell had 4 players who scored over ten points, but Carolina had five and that was the decisive factor in the contest. Gerald Quick swished the nets for 20 points to lead the Camels in scoring.

CAMPBELL 55—WAKE FOREST FRESHMEN 92

Wake Forest was hot and Campbell was cold. Before the Camels could warm up the Baby Dea-

cons had too great a lead even for McCall's fighting five. Robert Adams was the big man for Campbell, getting 10 rebounds and 16 points.

CAMPBELL 69—LOUISBURG 71

A few seconds on the clock and a field goal made all the difference to 10 hustling players. The Camels were trailing by 3 at the half and ended up only 2 points behind the Hurricanes. Sonny Baker with 21 points and Robert Adams with 20 were the big guns for the Camels.

CAMPBELL 65—OAK RIDGE 50

The Camels came back from their last-second loss to Louisburg to defeat the Oak Ridge Cadets by 15 points. Sonny Baker collected 15 points for his night's work.

CAMPBELL 71—LOUISBURG 76

For the second time within a month, the Camels fell victim to Louisburg. Sonny Baker scored 17 points for the Camels.

CAMPBELL 85—E. M. I. 80

The Camels looked like true champions as they defeated E. M. I. in a high scoring contest. Robert Adams tossed in 19 points to lead the Camels' scoring.

CAMPBELL 89—McCRARY EAGLES 116

The Eagles were too much for the Camels to cope with, and beat them by a 116 to 89 margin. Jim Wiles and Sonny Baker each tallied 18 for Campbell.

CAMPBELL 67—WILMINGTON 108

Conference leading Wilmington handed the Camels a loss on the Seahawks' home court. Sonny Baker had 18 for the Camels; John Josephson was outstanding on defense.

CAMPBELL 66—WINGATE 65

The Camels got sweet revenge by beating Wingate 66 to 65 in a hard fought battle which wasn't decided until the final second. Ronnie Atkinson tossed in 16 points for the Camels.

Campbell 70—Chowan 50

Strong after their loss to Wilmington, the Camels defeated Chowan in a conference game by a score of 70 to 50. Sonny Baker was top man with 19 points while Jim Wiles was close behind with 15.

Campbell 59—Fredrick 61

The Camels suffered a 2-point defeat at the hands of Fredrick in a beginning-to-end thriller. John Josephson was the hero in defeat, grabbing 13 rebounds and scoring 17 points.

Campbell 87—Oak Ridge 69

Coach McCall's Camels defeated Oak Ridge for the second time this season. The Camels outplayed the Cadets from beginning to end for the win. Jim Wiles ripped the nets for 31 points.

Campbell 51—Wake Forest Freshmen 72

The Wake Forest Frosh handed the Camels a 72 to 51 defeat at Winston-Salem. Ronnie Atkinson and Jim Wiles played exceptional offense, tallying 16 points each.

Campbell 90—P. J. C. 66

For the second time this season Campbell defeated Presbyterian Junior College. Sonny Baker hit for 21 points for the conference victory.

Campbell 81—Wilmington 73

For the first time this season the Wilmington Seahawks were beaten. They were beaten by the hustling five from Campbell College. The Camels started strong and never once lost their poise to startle the Seahawks. Jim Wiles and Ronnie Atkinson hit for 24 points.

Campbell 49—Chowan 48

Campbell ended up on top of a season battle for another conference win. The win was led by Jim Wiles with 13 points and put Campbell into 3rd place.

Campbell finished 3rd in regular season play. Jim Wiles and Sonny Baker were selected to the All-Conference Team.

Basketball Tournament

BETTY BARNES
Tournament Queen

In the huddle

HONORS!
JIM WILES
All Tournament

Atta boy!

Campbell 56
Oak Ridge 43

Campbell 48
Fredrick 52

Ah, got it!

Campbell 99
Louisburg 86

Ronnie Ellis

Cheerleaders

Peggy Williford

Mary Ann Jernigan

Betsy Massey

Betsy Carroll
Chief

Stevie Starling

Nancy Harris

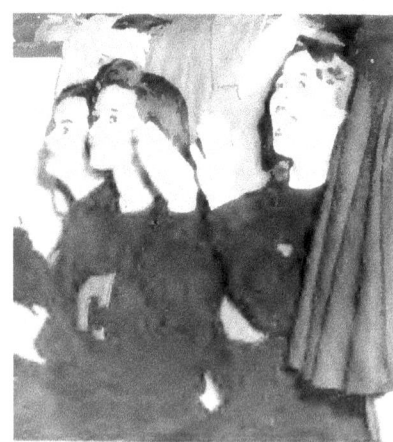

Ray Gilbert

Girls' Basketball

Front row, left to right: Jane Bryan, Marie Lewis, Frances Byrd, Linda Adams, Janice Vest, Sandy Bryan, Barbara Kelly. Second row, left to right: Hargrove Davis, Coach; Irene Blake, Sue Riddick, Anna McDaniel, Loretta Mitchell, Ruth Leary, Daphne Snell, Kay Gilden, Manager.

Sue Riddick and Barbara Kelly fight for rebound with Rex Girls.

Jane Bryan shoots for two!

Camelet Forwards

Front row, left to right: Daphne Snell, Barbara Kelly. *Second row, left to right:* Sue Riddick, Loretta Mitchell, Anna McDaniel, Frances Byrd.

Camelet Guards

Front row, left to right: Sandy Bryan, Janice Vest, Linda Adams. *Second row, left to right:* Jane Bryan, Irene Blake, Ruth Leary, Marie Lewis.

Coach Davis seems to be pointing out to a few of his second year girls, Daphne Snell, Irene Blake and Barbara Kelly that they went through the season like a breeze, winning 10 and losing only 1.

CAMPBELL 48—PINELAND 45

In the season's opener Coach Davis' Camelets turned back a strong Pineland team. Campbell was led by Marie Lewis and Jane Bryan, who tossed in 22 and 18 points respectively.

CAMPBELL 45—REX 40

With Marie Lewis and Jane Bryan leading the way with 25 and 13 points respectively, the Camelets were able to win their second straight game. Barbara Kelly and Sue Riddick were outstanding on defense.

CAMPBELL 48—HIGHSMITH 19

The Camelets started rolling in the early minutes of the game and did not slow down until the final buzzer. Marie Lewis was the offensive standout with 23 points; Daphne Snell was excellent on defense.

CAMPBELL 53—REX 49

For the second time this season the Camelets turned back Rex Hospital after a hard fight. Marie Lewis was practically the whole show for the Camelets, getting 32 points. Loretta Mitchell played exceptional defense.

CAMPBELL 40—PINELAND 48

The Pineland girls avenged an opening game defeat by handing the Camelets their first loss of the season. Marie Lewis scored 23 points for Campbell.

CAMPBELL 62—REX 45

For the third time this season the Camelets defeated the Rex Hospital nurses. Marie Lewis and Jane Bryan hit for 29 and 21 points respectively. Loretta Mitchell, Sue Riddick and Barbara Kelly were outstanding on defense.

CAMPBELL 78—FAYETTEVILLE 64

The Camelets won their sixth game of the season by turning back a very strong Fayetteville team. Marie Lewis tossed in 39 points to lead the Camelets.

CAMPBELL 57—HIGHSMITH 39

The Camelets made it two in a row over the Highsmith girls by beating them 57 to 39 for their seventh win of the season. Marie Lewis was the game's high scorer with 32 points.

CAMPBELL 89—VETVILLE 55

In scoring their eighth victory of the season the Camelets battered the Vetville girls 89 to 55. Marie Lewis tossed in an unbelievable 58 points and alone outscored Vetville.

CAMPBELL 75—FAYETTEVILLE 53

In winning their ninth game of the season the Camelets had a rather easy time. Marie Lewis scored 36 points while Jane Bryan tossed in 24. Sandy Bryan also tallied in double figures

I've got it!

Here I come, you better look out.

No—you can't hold it.

Homecoming

KATRINA CRUMPLER
High School Queen

JANICE VEST
Homecoming Queen

The Camels "hanged" and "buried" the Oak Ridge Cadets

1958 Baseball Team

First row, left to right: Gordon Welsh, Billy Byrd, Jimmie Bethune, Ronnie Atkinson, Harvey Walton, Manager; Jerry Wood, Glenwood Byrd, Sonny Challender, Dewin Johnson, Ray Burroughs. *Second row, left to right:* Hargrove Davis, Coach; Paul Cranmer, Wilbur Hargrove, Ronnie Johnson, Hugh Bazemore, Donald Wilson, Gerald Quick, Mark Prince, Junior Shelley, Elwood Bass, Manager.

SCORES

Campbell	15	E. M. I.	5
Campbell	6	Carolina Frosh	8
Campbell	11	Wingate	10
Campbell	0	Louisburg	7
Campbell	3	Chowan	1
Campbell	11	Pembroke	8
Campbell	2	P. J. C.	3
Campbell	6	P. J. C.	9
Campbell	0	Chowan	1
Campbell	6	Wilmington	10
Campbell	8	Louisburg	2
Campbell	3	Wilmington	9
Campbell	5	E. M. I.	4
Campbell	7	Carolina Frosh	5

1958 Tennis Team

Left to right: Charles Mace, Barton Tuck, Rufus Herring, Daniel Solomon, Andrew Terrill, Alva Terrill, Paul Powell.

1958 Golf Team

Left to right: Nick Porter, Johnny Marcin, Russell Ergood, Howard Turner, Leslie Wood, Bill Fisher.

TOM COLLINS
Intramural Director

For the second consecutive year, Pearson Dorm captured the intramural and Homecoming trophies. The volleyball and football championship teams were coached by Wilbur Hargrove. Receiving recognition for their outstanding participation in intramural sports activities were Paul Crammer, Julian Adams, Sonny Challender and Phil Harrell.

PEARSON DORM
VOLLEYBALL, SOUTHERN CONFERENCE AND SCHOOL FOOTBALL CHAMPIONS

First row, left to right: Tony Fashgo, Laurens Gaskins, Horace Gill, Charlie Johnson. *Second row, left to right:* Wilbur Hargrove, Claude Phillips, Roy Jones, David King, Gordon Welsh.

Intramural Sports

BRITT DORM

1st floor Britt won the Atlantic Coast Conference Championship and were runners-up for the school championship. *Left to right first row*: Frank Mayo, Eddie Pritchard, Edgar Little, Joel Chaney. *Second row*: Joe Earp, Dayton Capps, Carlyle Humphrey and Arthur Cobb.

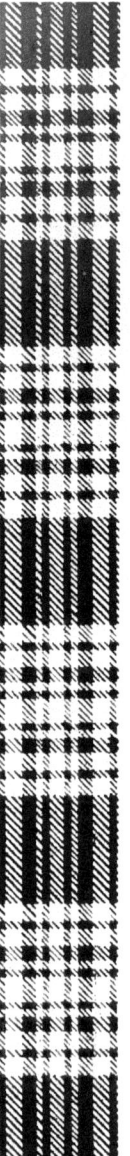

In Appreciation

A publication such as the PINE BURR *cannot be realized without the combined efforts of the student body, the faculty, and, in particular, the* PINE BURR *staff. To all those who took part in the common endeavor, I express my immeasurable appreciation.*

I am grateful to those called upon for singular contributions as warmly as I commend those of more extensive responsibility. Mr. King, our advisor, was a constant source of inspiration and encouragement. He has earned the gratitude of us all. I am truly indebted to our supporters and advertisers and to Mr. Haynes of Raleigh, who is responsible for the individual pictures, and to Mr. Charles Lee Smith of Edwards and Broughton Company, printers of the PINE BURR.

This has been a rewarding experience for me, and I have enjoyed working with each of you.

May good fortune be yours as you venture forward into the future.

MARY LEE CHILTON
Editor

Advertising

HAYNES' STUDIO
G. C. HAYNES, JR., *Proprietor*

OFFICIAL PHOTOGRAPHER
'59 ANNUAL

Member
The Photographers Association
of America

RALEIGH, N. C.

"HE IS ALREADY POVERTY STRICKEN
WHOSE HABITS ARE NOT THRIFTY"

GREETINGS TO CAMPBELL COLLEGE

BANK OF FUQUAY

"HOME OF SAVERS"

THE BANK OF FUQUAY ALWAYS PAYS THE HIGHEST RATE OF INTEREST ON SAVINGS ACCOUNTS THAT CAN BE PAID BY ANY BANK WITH DEPOSITS INSURED BY THE FEDERAL DEPOSIT INSURANCE CORPORATION. THE FIRST OF EVERY MONTH IS A NEW INTEREST PERIOD.

FUQUAY SPRINGS   and   CARY, N. C.

WE CARRY
A Complete Line of Nationally Advertised Brands

"THE

HOME

OF

BETTER

QUALITY"

RAY'S LADIES' STORE
Phone: 352-1   LILLINGTON, N. C.

PENGUIN

FROZEN AND CANNED FOODS

RALEIGH, N. C.

We Carry a Complete Line of Quality
Frozen and Canned Foods

Phone TEmple 2-2035

PATTERSON'S PACKING CO.

CONGRATULATIONS

TO CLASS OF 1959

Patterson's Label Is Your Assurance

of Finest Quality in

Franks, Sausages, Chili, and

Other Meat Products.

PATTERSON'S PACKING CO.

SANFORD, N. C.

Meredith College

Fully accredited liberal arts college. Departments of art, business, home economics, music. Supervised teaching in city schools. Progressive educational program in terms of Christian character and leadership. Distinguished record of student honors and achievement. Attractive location in "The Educational Center of the State." 170-acre campus. Modern fireproof dormitories. $2,250,000 Expansion Program in progress.

Write for Catalogue

CARLYLE CAMPBELL, *President*

RALEIGH, NORTH CAROLINA

Compliments

of

PIEDMONT

COFFEE

SERVICE

Box 2112

DURHAM, NORTH CAROLINA

Congratulations and Best Wishes
to the
Graduating Class of 1959

**ADAMS CONCRETE
PRODUCTS CO.**

FUQUAY - VARINA
and
DURHAM, N. C.

Producers of Concrete Masonry
and Ready Mix Concrete

**INSTITUTIONAL FOODS
COMPANY, INC.**

Box 9147

RALEIGH, N. C.

COMPLIMENTS

**IRA W. DAY—
RICHARD C. DAY**

General Agents
Security Life & Trust Co.

Raleigh, N. C.

Estate Planning
Business & Group Insurance

We handle the Group Life Plan for Campbell College and would be glad to advise individuals about their personal programs.

Stephenson's Soda & Sundry Shop
IN BUIES CREEK
COMPLETE LINE OF SCHOOL SUPPLIES
STATIONERY - COSMETICS - CANDY

Open 7:00 A.M. - 9:00 P.M.
Mon.-Sat.

Students Always Welcome

TILLEY AND MATTHEWS

*Seeds, Feeds, and Fertilizers
Paint and Farm Supplies
Maytag Appliances*

LIQUID NITROGEN SOLUTIONS

Phone MU 7-5202   -:-   P. O. Box 407
FUQUAY SPRINGS, N. C.

CROSS POULTRY COMPANY

MILK FED POULTRY

Live and Dressed

•

RALEIGH, N. C.

FIRST-CITIZENS BANK & TRUST CO.

ESTABLISHED 1898

Serving North Carolina
With Complete Banking
& Trust Services

Member Federal Deposit Insurance Corporation

SMITHFIELD

One to grow on...

Good health is our business. We take a deep personal pride in watching the growth and development of youngsters raised on Pine State's good, health-giving milk and dairy foods. We feel great satisfaction in the knowledge that we contribute to the growth of the community as we do to the growth of its citizens.

We're proud of the fact that we're growing, too... that more and more families are asking for Pine State's pure, delicious milk, ice cream and other fine dairy foods.

North Carolina's Choice Since 1919

Pine State

WATSON SEAFOOD & POULTRY COMPANY

RALEIGH, N. C.

Phone TE 2-5846

•

POULTRY - SEAFOOD

PORTION MEATS

BEEF - VEAL - PORK

Bullock's Barb-Q Place

Hillsboro Rd. - U.S. 70-A

DURHAM, N. C.

Barb-Q, Brunswick Stew,
Fried Chicken & Seafood

Phone 8-6211

Mr. and Mrs. W. G. Bullock, Props.

MORE NATIONALLY ADVERTISED
FASHIONS THAN ANY STORE
IN EASTERN CAROLINA

HUDSON-BELK CO.

RALEIGH

"Eastern Carolina's Largest Store"

Phone MU 7-4666

JOHNSON'S DRUG STORE

The Store of Personal Service

•

FUQUAY SPRINGS, N. C.

TWIN CITY LAUNDRY & CLEANERS

SANITONE

Beautifully Finished Shirts

1-Day Service On Request

New and Improved Sanitone
Dry Cleaning

FUQUAY SPRINGS, N. C.

NEW YORK LIFE INSURANCE COMPANY

J. A. OVERTON, REPRESENTATIVE

"Insurance Service in This Community Since 1924"

Life, Annuities, Accident
Sickness, Group
and Educational

323 Vance Street   Phone Spring 3-5852
SANFORD, NORTH CAROLINA

BYRD'S DRIVE-IN

Fine Foods

★

1 Mile South, New 401 Highway
RALEIGH, N. C.

K & L AUTO SERVICE

WE SELL NEW AND USED AUTO, TRUCK AND
TRACTOR PARTS, STRUCTURAL STEEL
AND STEEL PRODUCTS
WE BUY SCRAP IRON & METAL
WE SELL NEW AND USED STEEL

GARNER ROAD   P. O. Box 2042
DIAL TE 2-3312 - TE 2-4193

FILES   DESKS

CAPITAL PRINTING COMPANY, INC.

RALEIGH, NORTH CAROLINA

Distinctive Furniture

Quality Printing

SAFES   CHAIRS

Compliments of

T. R. ASHWORTH, INC., Dist.

Gulf Oil Products

TIRES

TIRE RECAPPING

FUQUAY SPRINGS, N. C.

Compliments of

Mother and Daughter STORES, INC.

•

INSURANCE BUILDING
RALEIGH, N. C.

YOUR GUARANTEE OF SATISFACTION
- PAINTS
- L. P. GAS
- FURNITURE
- TELEVISION
- GAS AND ELECTRIC APPLIANCES
- BONDED MATTRESSES

JOHNSON COTTON COMPANY
DUNN, N. C., and Affiliated Stores

Cromartie Funeral Home PHONE 2077 DUNN, NORTH CAROLINA	**Finer Diner** *of Lillington* ● A NICE PLACE TO EAT
Compliments of Fair Bluff Milling Co., Inc. FAIR BLUFF, N. C.	**HUDSON-BELK CO.** FUQUAY SPRINGS Phone 300
HERFF-JONES CO. INDIANAPOLIS, INDIANA *Class Rings, Invitations, Personal Cards* C. A. JACKSON, JR., *Representative* Route 5 DUNN, N. C.	Johnson's Registered Jewelers *American Gem Society* *Catering to Brides* 309 Fayetteville St. RALEIGH, NORTH CAROLINA *Congratulations to Graduates*
KELLY'S DRUG STORE For Prescriptions PHONE 2751 LILLINGTON, N. C.	STROUD PONTIAC 420-422 N. Main Street Telephones: Office 500; Service 541 ● FUQUAY SPRINGS, N. C.

ASHWORTH'S, INC. CLOTHING & SHOES DOBBS HATS GRIFFON SUITS FLORSHEIM SHOES VAN HEUSEN SHIRTS *Completely Air Conditioned* FUQUAY SPRINGS, N. C.	**BALENTINES** RESTAURANT ★ 315 Fayetteville Street Raleigh, N. C.
THE COUNTY PRESS Printers of "*Creek Pebbles*," Campbell College Newspaper BENSON, N. C. Phone 256-1	*Compliments of* **HOOD'S DRUG STORE** "*Prescription Specialist*" Phone 2348 DUNN, N. C.
ELLIOTT'S PHARMACY Drug Service Since 1914 Phone MU 7-2277 Fuquay Springs, N. C.	W. C. Stuart Phone 416 Wallace J. Stuart **THE GROCERTERIA** Groceries Fresh Meats - Fruits - Vegetables P. O. Box 667 Fuquay Springs, N. C.
SANITARY CLEANERS TOP QUALITY CLEANERS DIAL 4311 LILLINGTON, N. C.	G.E. Home Appliances and G.E. Television **WILBOURNE FURNITURE COMPANY** LILLINGTON and DUNN

COMPLIMENTS OF

ROGERS ESSO SERVICE
Fuquay Springs, N. C.

THE MEN'S STORE
Dunn, N. C.

CITY MARKET
Lillington, N. C.

BYRD'S FLOWER SHOP
Fuquay-Varina

BROCK CHEVROLET CO.
Lillington, N. C.

COLLEGE CAFE

"Pop's Place"

Specialties:
French Fries, Hamburgers,
and
Hamburger Steaks

*

BUIES CREEK, N. C.

Roster

Abernathy, Robert Smith
Route 1
Fuquay Springs, N. C.

Abrams, James Louis
Route 1
Macclesfield, N. C.

Adams, Bill J.
Route 2
Angier, N. C.

Adams, Jeffrey Lynn
Route 1
Newton Grove, N. C.

Adams, Linda Faye
Route 2
Dunn, N. C.

Adams, Joel R.
Route 2
Angier, N. C.

Adams, Robert A.
210 2nd Street
Clayton, N. C.

Adams, Roy Lee
Route 2
Angier, N. C.

Adams, Julian Frederick, Jr.
921 N. Blount St.
Raleigh, N. C.

Adcock, Starlon Willis
Box 193
Lillington, N. C.

Aiken, Charles Linville
1602 East Geer Street
Durham, N. C.

Ali, Kamil Abbas
Buie's Creek, N. C.

Almy, Katherine Elizabeth
330 Phoenix Avenue
Daytona Beach, Florida

Alphin, Clara Lynda
Route 2
Mt. Olive, N. C.

Altman, Betty Sue
Route 1
Coats, N. C.

Altman, Frances Jeanette
122 West Main Street
Benson, N. C.

Ammons, Henry Walter
Route 1
Dunn, N. C.

Ammons, Mary Jan
Route 2, Box 52
Lumberton, N. C.

Anderson, Gene Randall
Old Snow Hill Road
Kinston, N. C.

Anderson, Leonard Eldridge
Franklin Street
Enfield, N. C.

Andrews, Lee Earl
208 Chestnut Street
Lexington, N. C.

Angell, Don Gray
Route 2
East Bend, N. C.

Angell, Myron Mooney
Route 3
Mocksville, N. C.

Arasta, Houshang
Buie's Creek, N. C.

Arasta, Manucher
Buie's Creek, N. C.

Ashworth, John
Buie's Creek, N. C.

Atkins, Waverly Eugene
1111 Wautauga Street
Raleigh, N. C.

Atkinson, Ronald Robert
15 Scott Street
Riverside, New Jersey

Auld, David Bruce
1800 Forrest Road
Durham, N. C.

Ausley, Andrew Harold
West Bay Street
Dunn, N. C.

Autry, William Seymore
Route 1
Stedman, N. C.

Avery, Larry Earl
Route 1
Erwin, N. C.

Avery, Roy Leon
Route 4, Box 389
Dunn, N. C.

Aycock, Edward Gordon
Box 133
Micro, N. C.

Baggett, John Dalton
604 University Drive
Greensboro, N. C.

Bagley, Worth Wrenn
Route 2
Kenly, N. C.

Bagwell, Larry K.
Buie's Creek, N. C.

Bailey, Conrad Ziegler, Jr.
702 West Main Street
Elizabeth City, N. C.

Baird, Carlton Edward
Route 1, Box 31-C
Roanoke Rapids, N. C.

Baird, Ronald Sims
528 Harris Street
Roanoke Rapids, N. C.

Baker, Charles Winfred
1112 Horton Road
Durham, N. C.

Baker, Everett Norman
Route 1
Broadway, N. C.

Baker, Neil Duncan
Box 4
Rowland, N. C.

Baker, Sidney W.
Hyde Park Avenue
Durham, N. C.

Blackmann, Carl J.
60 Davie Circle
Chapel Hill, N. C.

Balentine, John Warren
2712 Anderson Drive
Raleigh, N. C.

Ballard, Curtis Lane
Route 2
Fuquay Springs, N. C.

Barbee, Joseph Fields
Route 1
Maysville, N. C.

Barbrey, Gabriel Joseph
William Street
Clinton, N. C.

Barefoot, Barbara Ann
Route 2
Four Oaks, N. C.

Barefoot, Betsy Leigh
Route 2
Four Oaks, N. C.

Barefoot, Judy Catherine
Route 5
Dunn, N. C.

Barefoot, Robert Edward
Route 1
Benson, N. C.

Barefoot, Waylon A.
Holmes Street
Benson, N. C.

Barfield, Bobby Gene
604 Williams Street
Clinton, N. C.

Barfield, William Pope
110 N. King Avenue
Dunn, N. C.

Barlow, Leonard Hall, Jr.
1400 Central Drive
Kannapolis, N. C.

Barnes, Bettie June
Rt. 1
Jacksonville, N. C.

Barnes, Linda Faye
Rt. 4
Lumberton, N. C.

Barnes, Richard Joseph
604 Clyde Avenue
Wilson, N. C.

Bass, Bobby Ray
Route 1, Box 320
Four Oaks, N. C.

Bass, William Elwood
Route 1
Four Oaks, N. C.

Batts, James Howard
300 Summit Avenue
Kinston, N. C.

Baucom, William B.
Buie's Creek, N. C.

Baughn, Sandra Louise
Box 173
West End, N. C.

Beale, Carolyn Marie
Route 1
Lillington, N. C.

Beck, Larry Eugene
Box 44
Kinston, N. C.

Bennett, Mary Zillah
Route 1
Ash, N. C.

Berry, Robert Claiborne
111 Second Avenue
Durham, N. C.

Best, Ben Gray
Route 3
Dunn, N. C.

Best, George Robert, III
821 West 5 Avenue
Lexington, N. C.

Best, Joe Cephus
Route 1
Goldsboro, N. C.

Best, Tommy Randall
407 North Herman
Goldsboro, N. C.

Beverly, Richard Donald
Route 4
Conway, S. C.

Bishop, Nathan Marvin, III
517 Jackson Street
Durham, N. C.

Bissette, Rex Autry
Route 2
Middlesex, N. C.

Blackwell, Barbara Ann
Route 2
Virgilina, Va.

Blackwell, Betty Jean
Route 4
Oxford, N. C.

Blake, Peggy Irene
Route 3, Box 34
Rockingham, N. C.

Bland, John H.
1014 Sunset Avenue
Rocky Mount, N. C.

Blowe, Jewel Anne
Boykins, Va.

Boggess, Ann Howard
207 Kenneth Blvd.
Havelock, N. C.

Boggs, Jean Ann
251 Alton Avenue
Dayton, Ohio

Bond, Grace Jean
Buie's Creek, N. C.

Bond, William Keith
Anderson Street
Selma, N. C.

Bordeaux, Grady Asbury
Route 1, Box 102
Elizabethtown, N. C.

Bowers, Thurman David
Route 4, Box 132
Greensboro, N. C.

Bowling, Lee Roy
Route 1
Aberdeen, N. C.

Bowling, Willie Jean
Lillington, N. C.

Brackney, Kennard Samuel
4815 66th Place
Hyattsville, Maryland

Bradshaw, Edward Neil
320 Avon Drive
Raleigh, N. C.

Brantley, Erastus Clifford, Jr.
Route 2
Zebulon, N. C.

Brauns, William Erwin
1009 W. Wendover Avenue
Greensboro, N. C.

Bridger, Robert Craven
Box 325
Bladenboro, N. C.

Briggs, Jenny Lillian
Route 1
Leasburg, N. C.

Briggs, Thomas W.
Buie's Creek, N. C.

Briley, George Henry
Route 5, Box 86
Greenville, N. C.

Briley, James Kirk
Route 1
Stokes, N. C.

Brite, Miles Jessup
Route 2
Elizabeth City, N. C.

Britt, Betty Anne
1912 East 5th Street
Lumberton, N. C.

Britt, Henry Forest
209 Market Street
Fairmont, N. C.

Britt, Robert Edward
605 Carthage Road
Lumberton, N. C.

Broadway, Murrell Ray
910 Edwards Street
Kinston, N. C.

Brooks, David Eugene
Route 1
Bath, N. C.

Brooks, Gene Terrell
Box 1161
Albemarle, N. C.

Brooks, Tommy George
Wallace, N. C.

Brown, Billie Dean
1009 W. Broad Street
Dunn, N. C.

Brown, Carolyn Beatrice
Route 1
Lillington, N. C.

Brown, Charles Franklin, Jr.
Hope Mills, N. C.

Brown, Dencie Kay
Route 2
Lillington, N. C.

Brown, Loraine Frances
Mamers, N. C.

Brown, Louise
Box 615
Dunn, N. C.

Brown, Terry Winston
Four Oaks, N. C.

Brown, Wanda Lynne
Stacy, N. C.

Bryan, Alex Gray
Route 1
Jacksonville, N. C.

Bryan, James Stedman Black
307 Valley Road
Fayetteville, N. C.

Bryan, Lois Ann
Route 5, Box 392
Lumberton, N. C.

Bryan, Sandra Leigh
Route 1
Chinquapin, N. C.

Bryan, Thelma Jane
Route 2
Bladenboro, N. C.

Bryant, Billy Martin
Route 2
Carthage, N. C.

Bryant, Robert Small
Buie's Creek, N. C.

Buchanan, John Wesley
Broadway, N. C.

Buchanan, Phil K., Jr.
Buie's Creek, N. C.

Buchanan, William Watkins
Route 2
Roxboro, N. C.

Buffaloe, Billy Bryant
820 Garner Road
Garner, N. C.

Bullard, Mary Fern
Box 71
Chadbourn, N. C.

Bullard, Willis Monroe
Buie's Creek, N. C.

Bunce, Jimmy
Route 3
Fayetteville, N. C.

Bunn, Sarah Ann
118 E. Vernon Avenue
Wake Forest, N. C.

Burden, James Roscoe
Aulander, N. C.

Burgner, Foster Cline
1513 Page Street
Durham, N. C.

Burns, Weyland S.
Buie's Creek, N. C.

Burroughs, James B
Buie's Creek, N. C.

Burton, Ora Echol, Jr.
417 Jasmine Street
Clearwater, Florida

Butler, Robert M.
Route 1
Clinton, N. C.

Butler, William Adam
Route 1
Clinton, N. C.

Butts, James Clellon
Route 1
Lillington, N. C.

Byrd, Benjamin Sherwood
Route 1
Smithfield, N. C.

Byrd, Billy Dale
Buie's Creek, N. C.

Byrd, Billie Jean
Route 1
Coats, N. C.

Byrd, David Lincoln
Route 1, Box 246
Chadbourn, N. C.

Byrd, Elizabeth Lee
201 East James Street
Lillington, N. C.

Byrd, Frances Worth
Route 7
Sanford, N. C.

Byrd, Hubert Glenwood
Route 1
Coats, N. C.

Byrd, James Ronald
Route 3
Lillington, N. C.

Byrd, Josiah Reynolds
Box 27
Bunnlevel, N. C.

Byrd, Lawrence Hazel, Jr.
6 Ocean Blvd.
Myrtle Beach, S. C.

Byrd, Neil Allen
Bunnlevel, N. C.

Byrd, Patricia Lane
Route 1
Coats, N. C.

Byrd, Robert Gentry
Buie's Creek, N. C.

Byrum, Betty Jane
Route 1
Edenton, N. C.

Callihan, James Clarence
P. O. Box 147
Clarkton, N. C.

Camecho, Juan
Buie's Creek, N. C.

Cameron, Charlotte Sue
201 N. 9th Street
Erwin, N. C.

Cameron, Judy Erwin
Kipling, N. C.

Campbell, William Vance
142 West Acadin Avenue
Winston-Salem, N. C.

Capps, Betty Freeman
Route 2
Lucama, N. C.

Capps, Dayton
810 17th Avenue
Conway, S. C.

Carr, Eugene Bryan
Route 1
Godwin, N. C.

Carr, James Thomas
Route 1
Carrsville, Virginia

Carr, Jerry Thomas
Route 1
Godwin, N. C.

Carroll, Betty Lou
2005 N. Fayetteville St.
Asheboro, N. C.

Carter, Roger Walter
Route 5
Sanford, N. C.

Carter, Samuel Patrick
Buie's Creek, N. C.

Carter, William Eugene
219 South Main Street
Raeford, N. C.

Castelloe, Raleigh Roosevelt
Route 2
Windsor, N. C.

Caudle, John William
Route 2, Box 60
Leaksville, N. C.

Challender, Raymond Howard, Jr.
Magnolia Road
Pemberton, New Jersey

Chance, Roy Louis
Route 1
Parkton, N. C.

Chaney, William Joel
1404 Barnes Street
Reidsville, N. C.

Chappell, Dan Motley
Route 1
Fuquay Springs, N. C.

Cheaves, Nancy Rose
Box 353
Spring Hope, N. C.

Chilton, Mary Lee
Moseley, Virginia

Churchill, Joyce Anne
6931 Emerson Street
Hyattsville, Maryland

Chvich, Melvin Raymond
43 Canton Road
Wintersville, Ohio

Clapp, Ronald Charles
121 East Main Street
Swepsonville, N. C.

Clark, Gordon William
Route 7
Sanford, N. C.

Clark, Joyce Ellen
Rocky Point, N. C.

Clayton, Joy Dan
Route 2
Angier, N. C.

Clemmons, Irving Thomas, Jr.
Route 2, Box 250
Leland, N. C.

Clifton, Gerald Thomas
Route 1
Faison, N. C.

Coats, Charles William
Route 1
Angier, N. C.

Cobb, Arthur Wesley
Route 1
Reidsville, N. C.

Colley, Thomas Jack, Jr.
M O Q 2312
Camp Lejeune, N. C.

Collie, Robert Carr
73 Falls Road Ext.
Rocky Mount, N. C.

Collins, Bobby Carlton
Route 1
Whiteville, N. C.

Collins, Charlie Wayland
Corban Court Apartments
Concord, N. C.

Collins, Hugh George, Jr.
Lake View Road
Fairmont, N. C.

Colville, Harold Eugene
Route 1
Bunnlevel, N. C.

Cook, Evelyn Virginia
Calypso, N. C.

Cooke, James Constant
1535 Barnes Street
Reidsville, N. C.

Cooper, Donald Paul
Route 2
Hillandale Road
Durham, N. C.

Cooper, Donald Raymond
Route 1
Cary, N. C.

Cooper, Nancy Glover
402 East "H" Street
Erwin, N. C.

Corbett, Fred L.
Buie's Creek, N. C.

Corrales, Eneyda Fuentes
Buie's Creek, N. C.

Corrales, Jaime Flientes
Buie's Creek, N. C.

Cotton, Donald Gene
1104 Gorman Street
Raleigh, N. C.

Coughenour, Richard N., Jr.
205 Cochran Avenue
Fayetteville, N. C.

Courie, Raymond Taft
605 College Street
Kinston, N. C.

Crabtree, William, Jr.
Erwin Road
Dunn, N. C.

Cranmer, Paul Irving
38 Elizabeth Street
Pemberton, New Jersey

Crawford, Larry Joe
202 East Markham Street
Durham, N. C.

Crawley, William Charles
1700 Fairview Road
Raleigh, N. C.

Creech, Billy Ann
Route 2
Princeton, N. C.

Creech, Carson, Vasco
Parrish Drive
Benson, N. C.

Creech, Marion Farrior
Box 476
Buie's Creek, N. C.

Creede, Jean
502 Kirkland
Greensboro, N. C.

Crisp, Amos Mancel, III
Box 303
Pinetops, N. C.

Crissman, Patsy Lou
Route 2
Fuquay Springs, N. C.

Cromartie, Meredith Sue
North Orange Avenue
Dunn, N. C.

Crumpler, Vernon Ray
1125 Sunset Avenue
Clinton, N. C.

Cunningham, Ronald Owen
560 S. 5th Avenue
Kankakee, Illinois

Curle, William Edward
311 Sherwood Place
Kinston, N. C.

Curtis, Jean Audrey
English Street
Thomasville, N. C.

Curtiss, Kenneth George
1810 Saint Mary's Street
Raleigh, N. C.

Daniel, Clara Priscilla
Route 1
Rougemont, N. C.

Daniels, Jerry Reece
2204 Francis Street
High Point, N. C.

Darnell, Betty Jo
Bolivia, N. C.

Daughtridge, Joseph Garland
1100 Sycamore Street
Rocky Mount, N. C.

Daughtry, Dallie Preston
Route 1
Faison, N. C.

Daughtry, James Elton
Route 1
Smithfield, N. C.

Daughtry, Ludie Jacqueline
Route 3
Clinton, N. C.

Davis, Eric Carlton
Route 1
Raleigh, N. C.

Davis, Linda Jane
Route 1
Evergreen, N. C.

Davis, Roland Bowden
Route 1
Seven Springs, N. C.

Davis, Wayland Thomas
Route 1
Albertson, N. C.

Dawson, Marvin Henry
2330 Huron Cr.
Durham, N. C.

Day, David Alexander
Murfreesboro, N. C.

Dean, Benjamin Franklin
Box 253
Buie's Creek, N. C.

Dechent, Anne Jones
Route 1
Goldsboro, N. C.

Dechent, James Howe
Buie's Creek, N. C.

DeLappe, Brenda Ruth
309 Richardson Street
Ambassador Apts. No. 2
High Point, N. C.

DeMent, Ebbie Ruppert
Route 5
Oxford, N. C.

Dement, Garvis Mason
Route 1
Holly Springs, N. C.

Dennis, Charlotte Faye
Route 1
Holly Springs, N. C.

Denton, Hubert Macon
Route 2
Nashville, N. C.

Dew, James Robert
Route 4
Whiteville, N. C.

Dewberry, Geraldine Mercedes
3642 Roland Avenue
Baltimore, Md.

Dewberry, Willis Elbert
3642 Roland Avenue
Baltimore, Md.

Dixon, Judy Lynn
Morgan Street
Benson, N. C.

Dixon, Royal Hunter
Route 1
Clayton, N. C.

Dodson, Jerry Dean
913 Mantle Street
Mt. Airy, N. C.

Dorman, Carolynn McLamb
112 Joy Street
Dunn, N. C.

Dorman, Donnie Gene
Route 1
Coats, N. C.

Douglas, Don Kelley
306 N. Mendenhall Street
Greensboro, N. C.

Dowd, William Carey
2516 Kenmore Drive
Raleigh, N. C.

Drake, Thomas Franklin
Route 7
Raleigh, N. C.

Draughon, David Dixon
Cumberland, N. C.

Draughon, Robert Taylor
Route 4
Zebulon, N. C.

Drawdy, George Ellis
Buie's Creek, N. C.

Duke, Robert Byrd
903 12th Avenue
Conway, S. C.

Duncan, Guy
Route 2
Nichols, N. C.

Duncan, Thomas Sherrill
Route 2
Angier, N. C.

Duncan, Thomas S.
Buie's Creek, N. C.

Dunn, Billie Lou
Route 5
Raleigh, N. C.

Dunn, Claud Lee
Route 3
Zebulon, N. C.

Dupree, Ornettie Catherine
Route 1
Smithfield, N. C.

Dupree, Nancy Louise
Route 1
Angier, N. C.

Eakes, Evelyn Louise
Route 1
Oxford, N. C.

Earnhardt, Martha Gale
307 W. Canary Street
Dunn, N. C.

Earp, George A.
Winnabow, N. C.

Earp, Joe Thomas
Box 617
Angier, N. C.

Easterling, Ann Elizabeth
P. O. Box 103
Hartsville, S. C.

Eddins, Henry Thomas
Route 5, Box 350
Durham, N. C.

Edmonds, Olivia Lee
P. O. Box 264
Hobgood, N. C.

Edwards, Johnny Brooks
Main 76
Fair Bluff, N. C.

Edwards, Nancy Jane
Route 1
Princeton, N. C.

Edwards, Virgil James
Route 3, Box 736
Craven, N. C.

Eichhorn, Charles W.
5523 Wayne Road
Greensboro, N. C.

Elks, Helen Elizabeth
Route 2, Box 235
Goldsboro, N. C.

Ellen, Betty Lou
2045 South Drive
Jacksonville, N. C.

Ellen, Phillip Irvin
Angier, N. C.

Elliott, Maxine
Route 4
Oxford, N. C.

Elliott, Nancy Arlene
Route 2
Nichols, S. C.

Ellis, Johnnie Melvin
535 Fayetteville Street
Clayton, N. C.

Ellis, Ronald Gilliard, Jr.
308 Whitaker Mill
Raleigh, N. C.

Elmore, Thomas Vernon
1507 Peachtree Street
Goldsboro, N. C.

Ennis, Jackie O'Neal
503 W. Parrish Drive
Benson, N. C.

Enzor, Laura Anne
Route 1
Fair Bluff, N. C.

Ergood, Russell Merriel, III
180 Upland Way
Haddenfield, N. J.

Erwin, Betty Wrenn
West 6th Avenue
Lexington, N. C.

Estes, Margaret Olivia
115 Williams Street
Franklinton, N. C.

Evans, Ashby Dorsey, Jr.
209 Perry Street
Henderson, N. C.

Evans, Edward Robert
318 Church Street
Ahoskie, N. C.

Evans, James Arthur
Route 1, Box 295
Kenly, N. C.

Evans, John Lawrence
508 E. Church Street
Nashville, N. C.

Evans, Jonathan, Jr.
Route 5, Box 410
Fayetteville, N. C.

Ezzell, Robert Lee
Route 4
Whiteville, N. C.

Faily, Anwar Mohamad Ali
Buie's Creek, N. C.

Faircloth, James Keith
Route 1
Salemburg, N. C.

Faircloth, Rebecca Dunn
Route 1
Salemburg, N. C.

Faircloth, Willie
1700 E. Palm Street
Goldsboro, N. C.

Farrell, Paul E., Jr.
1208 Martindale Drive
Fayetteville, N. C.

Fastige, Anthony Nicholas
10 Friendship Place
Montclair, New Jersey

Fearing, Gordon Bradford
1108 Park Drive
Elizabeth City, N. C.

Ferrell, Ernest Hudson
2411 Knox Street
Durham, N. C.

Fields, Carl Edgar
Route 3
High Point, N. C.

Fields, Lacy Elwood
Route 5
Clinton, N. C.

Fisher, Billy R.
307 Main Street
Bladenboro, N. C.

Fisher, Frank Willis
P. O. Box 22
Battleboro, N. C.

Fisher, Janet Lee
Route 3
Lumberton, N. C.

Fisher, John White
Main Street
Battleboro, N. C.

Fisher, Mary Sue
802 Perry Street
Kinston, N. C.

Fisher, C. P. William
312 Woodland Avenue
Wake Forest, N. C.

Fleishman, Morton Theodore
1914 Morganton Road
Fayetteville, N. C.

Flowers, Charles Edward, Jr.
726 South Elam Avenue
Greensboro, N. C.

Flowers, Sibyl Whitehead
803 Raleigh Road
Ramseur, N. C.

Floyd, Billy Earl
710 Forrest Street
Raeford, N. C.

Fowler, Casey Syker, Jr.
1003 West 8th Street
Lillington, N. C.

Freeman, Judith Ann
West Parrish Drive
Benson, N. C.

French, William W., Jr.
Buie's Creek, N. C.

Futrell, Betty Lou
Route 2
Lucama, N. C.

Futrell, Isaac Gerald
Route 2
Lucama, N. C.

Gaines, John Alexander, Jr.
Route 1
Sanford, N. C.

Garcia, Agustin Pais
Buie's Creek, N. C.

Gardner, Sue Carolyn
211 South Eleanor Avenue
Dunn, N. C.

Garrard, Victor Gray
1801 Hillcrest Drive
Durham, N. C.

Garrell, Rufus Duke
Box 146
Tabor City, N. C.

Garrett, Ray Wayne
Moyock, N. C.

Garrett, Roy Lane
Moyock, N. C.

Gaskins, Laurens Maxwell, Jr.
2133 Weaver Street
Charleston, S. C.

Gaster, Marvin Edward
Route 8
Sanford, N. C.

Gentry, Kendall Francis, Jr.
Route 2
Roxboro, N. C.

Gentry, Nancy Louise
Boonville, N. C.

Gilbert, John Wayne
Route 3, Box 334
Rocky Mount, N. C.

Gilbert, Norman Ray
1244 Pamlico Drive
Greensboro, N. C.

Gilden, Myrtle Kay
Grandy, N. C.

Gill, Horace Thomas
Bullock, N. C.

Godbold, John Roberson
Route 3
Faison, N. C.

Godwin, Bobby Day
204 North Layton Avenue
Dunn, N. C.

Godwin, Homer Patrick, Jr.
2002 Erwin Road
Dunn, N. C.

Godwin, Wiley Norwood
Route 5
Dunn, N. C.

Godwin, William Jackie
Route 1
Clarendon, N. C.

Goodwin, Theda Ann
217 East Eden Street
Edenton, N. C.

Gore, J. D.
Route 1
Nakina, N. C.

Goss, Henry T., Jr.
208 East Geer Street
Durham, N. C.

Gove, Linda
206 North 10th Avenue
Dillon, S. C.

Grady, Edmund Lilly
1421 Morganton Road
Fayetteville, N. C.

Grady, Robert Shelton
Route 1
Albertson, N. C.

Grady, Theodore Kelly
Route 1
Albertson, N. C.

Graham, Henry White, Jr.
700 Hawkins Avenue
Sanford, N. C.

Graham, Sylvia Ann
Route 1
Broadway, N. C.

Gray, Havord Rham
Route 1
Jacksonville, N. C.

Gray, Tommy Nile
Route 1
Fuquay Springs, N. C.

Gray, Thomas Scott
1820 Arlington Street
Raleigh, N. C.

Green, Eldon Leo
Pine Street
Whiteville, N. C.

Greene, A. C., Jr.
1610 Brookside Avenue
Fayetteville, N. C.

Greene, Augustus Byron, Jr.
Route 5
Henderson, N. C.

Greene, Mrs. Carolyn Fuller
Box 164
Buie's Creek, N. C.

Gregory, Mary Frances
Buie's Creek, N. C.

Gresham, Geraldine Faison
2812 O'Berry Street
Raleigh, N. C.

Griffin, Annie Jo
Route 3
Louisburg, N. C.

Griffin, Barbara Ann
Route 2
Middlesex, N. C.

Griffin, Joe E.
Route 2
Fairmont, N. C.

Griffin, John Wayne
608 Greenland Street
Fayetteville, N. C.

Griffith, John Robert
Westover Avenue
South Hill, Virginia

Grimmer, Hubert Ray
213 Shirley Street
Tarboro, N. C.

Grubbs, Sylvia Faye
915 Bellevue Street
Burlington, N. C.

Gulledge, Margaret Lucile
Hawkins Street
Sanford, N. C.

Gurganus, Claudius Leach
Fifth Street
Smithfield, N. C.

Haddock, Robert Richard
Route 1
Holly Springs, N. C.

Haire, Kenneth Albert
Route 1
Varina, N. C.

Hales, John Bradley
Bladenboro, N. C.

Hall, George D., Jr.
Greenville, N. C.

Hall, George Rubin
608 South Boylan Avenue
Raleigh, N. C.

Hall, James Owen
Benson, N. C.

Hall, Robert Harold
Box 217
Holly Springs, N. C.

Hall, Robert Addison
426 North Cedar Street
Greensboro, N. C.

Hall, Stephen Cashwell
1701 High Street
New Bern, N. C.

Hamilton, Jessie Suggs
Route 4
Dunn, N. C.

Hammond, Charles Emory
Route 1
Linden, N. C.

Hammond, Ida Marie
Route 2
Nichols, S. C.

Hanchey, Anne
Wallace, N. C.

Hancock, Ernest Vernon, Jr.
808 North Church Street
Scotland Neck, N. C.

Hannon, Catherine Louisa
615 Dabney Drive
Henderson, N. C.

Harden, Joe Allen
Box 81
Bladenboro, N. C.

Hare, Jimmy Martin
Route 1
Lyner, N. C.

Hargrove, Wilbur Howard
Route 1, Box 158
Vincentown, New Jersey

Harper, Rom McCoy
Route 1
Pinkhill, N. C.

Harrell, Betty Ann
Route 3
Edenton, N. C.

Harrell, Carlisle W.
8621 Hammett Avenue
Norfolk, Virginia

Harrell, Robert Kelly
422 Mayeox Avenue
Norfolk, Virginia

Harrelson, Thomas Joseph
Caswell Avenue
Southport, N. C.

Harrington, Donald Lee
822 South Aycock Street
Greensboro, N. C.

Harrington, Donald Wayne
Box 75
Moncure, N. C.

Harrington, Janet Ann
Route 1
Broadway, N. C.

Harris, Charles Toby
Box 2502
Raleigh, N. C.

Harris, George Calvin
Route 2
Clayton, N. C.

Harris, Morgan Holt
Route 2, Box 188
Washington, N. C.

Harris, Nancy
3320 Kansas Avenue
Norfolk, Virginia

Harris, Reid Vick, II
Church Street
Seaboard, N. C.

Harris, William Sherrod, Jr.
208 Powell Street
Emporia, Virginia

Harrison, Gordon Marshall
110 Oak
Pocomoke, Maryland

Harvell, Donald Hoyle
Route 1
Willow Springs, N. C.

Hawes, Reuben Homer
Route 2
Rose Hill, N. C.

Hawkins, William L.
Route 5, Box 229
Petersburg, Virginia

Hayes, George Wayne
Route 2
Virgilina, N. C.

Hayes, William Green
1001 Southern Avenue
Fayetteville, N. C.

Henry, Earlene Gaye
601 South Orange Street
Dunn, N. C.

Henry, Geraldine Faye
601 South Orange Avenue
Dunn, N. C.

Henwood, Richard Sidney
205 North Dyer
Elizabeth City, N. C.

Hepler, Thomas Monroe, Jr.
Route 3
Winchester, Virginia

Hernandez, Rafael Romero
Buie's Creek, N. C.

Herndon, Alphus Sanders, Jr.
Route 4, Box 72
Durham, N. C.

Herring, Rufus Hilliary
607 College Street
Clinton, N. C.

Hicks, Bennie Ward
Route 3, Box 62
Nashville, N. C.

High, Cherrye Lane
Box 544
Middlesex, N. C.

Highsmith, Jerry Myers
813 Vermont
Smithfield, N. C.

Hill, Carolyn Dee
Fair Bluff, N. C.

Hill, Searlett Leigh
Route 1
Mount Olive, N. C.

Hilliard, Raymond Grant
Route 1, Box 75
Franklinville, N. C.

Hinson, Adolph
Route 1
Fair Bluff, N. C.

Hinson, Harry Lee, III
426 Arlington
Rocky Mount, N. C.

Hinton, William Kenneth
Route 4
Zebulon, N. C.

Hobbs, Cecil Wright, Jr.
Pleasant Street
Roseboro, N. C.

Hobbs, Judy Benton
Box 192
Aberdeen, N. C.

Hobbs, Lessie Jean
Bunnlevel, N. C.

Hobbs, Nell Brenda
Route 4
Raleigh, N. C.

Hobbs, Rodney Carroll
Route 1
Bunnlevel, N. C.

Hocutt, Benny Royster
Route 1
Wendell, N. C.

Hodges, Robert Wilson
1009 North Market Street
Washington, N. C.

Holder, Elwood Travis
Box 48
Mamers, N. C.

Holland, Harold Glenn
Route 1
Morrisville, N. C.

Holland, Perry Carlton
117 Carbonton Road
Sanford, N. C.

Holleman, Robert Dunn, Jr.
1110 Gregson Street
Durham, N. C.

Holt, Linda Marilyn
Albertson, N. C.

Holt, Ralph Edward, Jr.
901 West Trinity Avenue
Durham, N. C.

Homar, Donald Paul
723 Berryville Avenue
Winchester, Virginia

Hood, Eunice Doris
Box 118, Route 1
Rose Hill, N. C.

Horne, Walter Wells, Jr.
331 Princeton Street
Fayetteville, N. C.

Horrell, Mack Raymond
Route 1
Atkinson, N. C.

Horrell, Phil
Atkinson, N. C.

House, Brenda Joyce
Erwin, N. C.

House, James Merritt
South Lumber Street
Nashville, N. C.

House, Sharon Gail
305 East K Street
Erwin, N. C.

Howell, David Jack
2307 Fairview Road
Raleigh, N. C.

Howell, Lanny Mont
2319 Morganton Road
Fayetteville, N. C.

Howell, Phillip Rex
Route 1
Holly Springs, N. C.

Hudgins, William Stonecypher
Route 1
Bayside, Virginia

Hudson, Joel Blanney
217 Moore Street
Clinton, N. C.

Hudson, Percy Carter
Route 5
Dunn, N. C.

Hughes, Elmond Lee
Buie's Creek, N. C.

Hughes, Patsy Elizabeth
Route 2
Oxford, N. C.

Humphrey, Carlyle Paul
Shannon, N. C.

Humphrey, C. W.
Route 1
Kinston, N. C.

Humphries, James Paul
1615 Rose Street
Goldsboro, N. C.

Hunt, Walter Skellie
1606 Canterbury Road
Raleigh, N. C.

Hunt, William Taylor
Route 2
Grifton, N. C.

Hunter, Janice Pearl
Route 7
Sanford, N. C.

Hurst, Sara Lowder
9 Ruth Street
Jacksonville, N. C.

Hutchinson, Hoyt Phillip
Route 1
Nichols, N. C.

Jackson, Alice Lou
301 East Divine Street
Dunn, N. C.

Jackson, Cecile Kay
1108 Cherry Street
Tarboro, N. C.

Jackson, Joe Wade
881 Southern Avenue
Fayetteville, N. C.

Jackson, John Thomas, Jr.
Route 2
Dunn, N. C.

Jackson, Lynn Randall
Route 2
Beulaville, N. C.

Jacobs, Lewis George
Buie's Creek, N. C.

James, Charles Henry
Route 4
Elizabeth City, N. C.

Jenkins, Lee Bryant
108 Park Avenue
Kinston, N. C.

Jenkins, Robert Hobgood
Zebulon, N. C.

Jennings, Bobby Lee
211 Ebringhaur Street
Elizabeth City, N. C.

Jennings, Mary Louise
1114 W. Williams Circle
Elizabeth City, N. C.

Jernigan, Glen Reginald
1823 Wilmont Road
Charlotte, N. C.

Jernigan, Mary Ann
Thornedale Drive
Oxford, N. C.

Jernigan, Robert Earl
Box 65
Dunn, N. C.

Jernigan, Robert Jessie
P. O. Box 675
Newport, N. C.

Johnson, Charles Astor
406 Hill Street
Benson, N. C.

Johnson, Charles Rockhil
102 Jervis Street
Pemberton, N. C.

Johnson, Epsie Jo-Ann
Route 2
Lumberton, N. C.

Johnson, Garland Henry
625 College Street
Jacksonville, N. C.

Johnson, Henry Pearl
502 E. Wilson Street
Farmville, N. C.

Johnson, Jimmy Waylon
Route 2
Four Oaks, N. C.

Johnson, Larry Eldon
State Hospital
Raleigh, N. C.

Johnson, Max Oliver
N. Lincoln Street
Benson, N. C.

Johnson, Reginald Allen
1104 S. Church Street
Burlington, N. C.

Johnson, Sherriel Lee
102 West 1 Street
Erwin, N. C.

Johnson, William Lee
Box 551
Roseboro, N. C.

Jones, Amorette Ione
Pudin Avenue
Pine Level, N. C.

Jones, Betty Ruth
3124 Fieldale Road
Greensboro, N. C.

Jones, Bobby R.
2319 Milburnie Road
Raleigh, N. C.

Jones, Crisman Snyder
1096 Nichols Drive
Raleigh, N. C.

Jones, James William
Route 1
Lillington, N. C.

Jones, Lewis Roy
Route 5
Oxford, N. C.

Jones, Vernon Walters
625 W. Club Blvd.
Durham, N. C.

Jones, William Lewis
Route 1
Farmville, N. C.

Jones, William Louis
1216 Mordecai Drive
Raleigh, N. C.

Jordan, Billy Charles
Crescent Beach, S. C.

Josephson, John Armstrong
Box 546
Asheville, N. C.

Kasha, Abdulwahid
Buie's Creek, N. C.

Keen, Joseph Weaver
Rich Square, N. C.

Kelly, Barbara Ann
117 Broughton Street
Garner, N. C.

Kelly, Gerald Rives
Route 1
Carthage, N. C.

Kelly, Jack Wayne
Route 4
Sanford, N. C.

Kelly, Joseph Harold
Route 4
Sanford, N. C.

Kenessey, Bela Anthony
Box 707
Kinston, N. C.

Kennedy, Bobby Faye
Biscoe, N. C.

Kennedy, Huey Ralph
Route 4
Goldsboro, N. C.

Kennedy, Troy Wayne
2930 Kennoah Drive
Winston-Salem, N. C.

Kennedy, Vernon Leonard
Route 5
Kinston, N. C.

Kennemur, Ann Courtney
624 Vance Street
Roanoke Rapids, N. C.

Kinch, Donald Ray
Raleigh, N. C.

King, Durward Elbert
206 Boxley Avenue
Suffolk, Virginia

King, David Wall
Route 3
Raleigh, N. C.

King, William Duvall
1914 Sunset Drive
Raleigh, N. C.

King, William Greene
Clinton, N. C.

Kirby, James Stanley
Route 1
Lucama, N. C.

Kirby, Michael Barfield
1001 Belmont Avenue
Fayetteville, N. C.

Kitchin, Mary Ellen
Central Avenue
Maxton, N. C.

Klugel, Sarah Yorkshire
506 Meherrin Street
Emporia, Virginia

Knight, Lee
Route 3, Box 39A
Fayetteville, N. C.

Knott, Carolyn Jean
Route 1
Fuquay Springs, N. C.

Kube, Delores Ann
6914 Freeport Street
Hyattsville, Maryland

Lackey, T. Lantz
Box 283
Buie's Creek, N. C.

Lamb, William Stacey
903 N. Oakum Street
Edenton, N. C.

Lancaster, George William
109 W. Center Street
Lexington, N. C.

Lane, Haywood A., Jr.
712 E. Walnut Street
Goldsboro, N. C.

Langston, Clara L.
Buie's Creek, N. C.

Lanier, Ernie Ray
Norwood Street
Wallace, N. C.

Lanier, Harvey Spencer
Route 2, Box 325
Leland, N. C.

Lanier, Walter Craven
Box 321
Lillington, N. C.

Lashley, Beverly Greene
Poplar Street
Angier, N. C.

Lasley, Charles Glenn
409 E. Virginia Avenue
Draper, N. C.

Lassiter, Hylah Cynthia
Potecasi, N. C.

Lassiter, Joseph Ralph
Route 3
Four Oaks, N. C.

Leary, Deborah Ruth
Route 1
Edenton, N. C.

Lee, Betty Ann
501 N. Fayetteville Avenue
Dunn, N. C.

Lee, Donell Raymard
500 S. Magnolia Avenue
Dunn, N. C.

Lee, Howard Monroe
410 S. McKay Avenue
Dunn, N. C.

Lee, Kenneth Monroe
Route 2
Benson, N. C.

Lee, Linda Allen
711 Cameron Drive
Kinston, N. C.

Lee, Peggy Gayle
Route 2
Benson, N. C.

Lee, Wade Thomas
Route 2
Four Oaks, N. C.

Lee, William Dalton
Box 131
Angier, N. C.

Lennon, Margaret Ruth
Route 2
Clarkton, N. C.

Leonard, Frances Adelaide
Route 2
Louisburg, N. C.

Lewis, Deanna Marie
Route 2
Middlesex, N. C.

Lewis, Kitty Margot
Route 1
Bolivia, N. C.

Little, Edgar Leroy
151 Glendale Avenue
Durham, N. C.

Little, Harold Lynn
214 Charlotte Avenue
Sanford, N. C.

Livengood, Max Robert
Route 3
Carthage, N. C.

Lyles, Jack Brown
Littleton, N. C.

Lynch, Rebecca Ann
Box 204
Chautauqua, N. C.

Lynch, James Mitchell
Warlich Street
Jacksonville, N. C.

Lynch, Robert Jack
Box 434
Apex, N. C.

Lynn, Daniel Carson
Franklin Road
Raleigh, N. C.

McBride, Herschel A.
1622 Gilmore Street
Fayetteville, N. C.

McCall, James Edward
1933 Williams Street
Greensboro, N. C.

McCormick, Archie Lockhart
Mills Home
Thomasville, N. C.

McCall, James Edward
Buie's Creek, N. C.

McCraw, Mary Elizabeth
Box 342
Cliffside, N. C.

McCullen, Garland Dan
Route 1
Faison, N. C.

McDaniel, Anna Justa
Route 3
Raleigh, N. C.

McDaniel, Fred Eugene
314 Churchill Drive
Fayetteville, N. C.

McDaniel, Herbert Alton
1013 9th Street
Durham, N. C.

McDonald, Jan Harlee
109 East G Street
Erwin, N. C.

McDonald, Lance Alexis
54 Maas Drive
Fort Bragg, N. C.

McDonald, Neill Angus
Raeford, N. C.

McDonald, William Eugene
Route 2
Lillington, N. C.

McGannon, William Edward
424 Shoteka Hill
Salem, Virginia

McGirt, Sarah Ellen
Astin Avenue
Maxton, N. C.

McGugan, David Brown
Route 3
Red Springs, N. C.

McIver, Wilbur LeRoy
1913 Glenwood Avenue
Raleigh, N. C.

McKenzie, Samuel N.
Wilmington, N. C.

McLamb, Barbara Ann
Route 1
Lillington, N. C.

McLamb, Edna Jean
Route 1
Wade, N. C.

McLamb, Joe E.
Route 1
Bunnlevel, N. C.

McLean, Rita Phyllis
904 Fairground Road
Dunn, N. C.

McLeod, David Gwin
307 Sylvan Road
Fayetteville, N. C.

McLeod, Jo Ann
Buie's Creek, N. C.

McMillan, Donald Alex
Pembroke, N. C.

McNeill, Andrew Patterson
Route 1
Broadway, N. C.

McPhail, Walter Alfred
Route 1
Dunn, N. C.

Macioce, Angelo
217 Bloomfield Avenue
Montclair, New Jersey

Mackey, Thomas Hughes
315 Hughes Street
Lancaster, S. C.

Macmillan, John Olive
310 Bradford Avenue
Fayetteville, N. C.

Maharg, Judith Ann
2550 Roanoke Avenue
Dayton, Ohio

Mann, Charles Lee
27 N. Lakeside Drive
Sanford, N. C.

Mann, Julian Turner, Jr.
411 South Layton Avenue
Dunn, N. C.

Marcin, John Michael
Box 995
Stuart, Florida

Mare, Charles Anthony
439 East 42nd Street
Brooklyn, New York

Marr, John Michael
201 Bethune Street
Fayetteville, N. C.

Marshall, Randall Tavner
Ruckersville, Virginia

Martin, Lynda Kay
327 New Bern Avenue
Raleigh, N. C.

Martin, Tony Gene
Route 1
Saint Pauls, N. C.

Mashburn, Roy E.
Hawkins Avenue
Sanford, N. C.

Mason, Alicia Ingram
355 East 2nd Avenue
Southern Pines, N. C.

Mason, Raymond Bruce
Route 1
Fuquay Springs, N. C.

Massengill, Alfred Wilburn
Box 296
Four Oaks, N. C.

Massengill, Linda Rachel
Route 1
Smithfield, N. C.

Massey, Betsy Ruth
Route 2
Zebulon, N. C.

Mathis, Alfred Ray
Warsaw, N. C.

Matthews, Barbara Jane
Route 1
Sanford, N. C.

Matthews, Braxton Ray
Kipling, N. C.

Matthews, Charles Jordan
Route 2
Nashville, N. C.

Matthews, Fred Lee
Route 2
Fuquay Springs, N. C.

Mauhsby, James Alton, Jr.
348 Hawley Lane
Fayetteville, N. C.

Maxwell, Grace Dare
607 West Pope Street
Dunn, N. C.

Maxwell, Hugh Gordon
1112 Evergreen Avenue
Goldsboro, N. C.

Maxwell, Sherrill Douglas
Falcon, N. C.

May, Hugh Randolph
Box 42
Anderson Arms Apt.
Dunn, N. C.

May, Julian Thorne
623 Eastern Avenue
Rocky Mount, N. C.

Mayo, David Whitley
Fremont, N. C.

Mayo, Frank Taylor
122 Winstead Road
Rocky Mount, N. C.

Meade, Herbert Franklin
607 South Elam Avenue
Greensboro, N. C.

Meade, James Franklin
35 Crooked Billet
Hatboro, Pennsylvania

Medlin, Gerald Wayne
Route 8
Sanford, N. C.

Medlin, Thomas LaVerne
610 Sasser Street
Raleigh, N. C.

Mercer, Carrie Lou
Route 1
Wilson, N. C.

Mercer, Walter Kenith
1006 Desmond Street
Kinston, N. C.

Merritt, Billy Charles
1509 Old Wilson Road
Rocky Mount, N. C.

Merritt, Margaret Alice
Garfield Road
Burlington, N. C.

Metcalf, William H.
412 North Wilmington Street
Raleigh, N. C.

Midgett, Luke Bradshaw, Jr.
203 Chamberlain Street
Raleigh, N. C.

Midkiff, John Walter
Route 2
Mount Airy, N. C.

Miller, Bobby Ray
Route 1
Benson, N. C.

Miller, Nancy Irene
Route 1
Beulaville, N. C.

Milton, David Fleming
Route 1, Box 190
Lillington, N. C.

Minnis, Jennie Faye
619 Harris Street
Burlington, N. C.

Minton, Shirley Jo
Route 1, Box 305 E
Suffolk, Virginia

Mitchell, Loretta Ann
Aulander, N. C.

Moeller, William Paul
2800 Sharon Road
Charlotte, N. C.

Molina, Mariano
Buie's Creek, N. C.

Montague, Margaret Ann
Route 2
Angier, N. C.

Montalva, Lydia
Paseo 653 Vedado
Havana, Cuba

Moore, Eugene Moses
1508 Charlotte Avenue
Kinston, N. C.

Moore, Henry Walton, Jr.
Hillsboro, N. C.

Moore, James Ballard
West Street
Cary, N. C.

Moore, James Robert, III
1221 Oakwood Drive
Rocky Mount, N. C.

Moore, William Davis
Box 673
Hillsboro, N. C.

Morgan, Carl Andrew
500 Howell Street
Rocky Mount, N. C.

Morgan, Claude VanBuren, Jr.
Route 3
Oxford, N. C.

Morgan, Eric Jason
Route 2
Spring Hope, N. C.

Morgan, Joseph Aubrey
Route 1
Fairmont, N. C.

Morgan, Joyce Alpin
Coats, N. C.

Morgan, Peggy Elaine
Route 1
Lillington, N. C.

Morris, Jimmy Austin
Route 1
Kenly, N. C.

Morris, Zeb A.
76 Angleside Drive
Concord, N. C.

Morton, Ronald Grey
503 North Endor
Sanford, N. C.

Mozingo, Garland Ray
Route 1
Goldsboro, N. C.

Mullen, Joel Benette
2301 Poole Road
Raleigh, N. C.

Murdock, William Henry, Jr.
1006 Gloria
Durham, N. C.

Murphy, James Irving
Zebulon, N. C.

Murrell, George Franklin
Route 5
Conway, S. C.

Nackley, Freed William
1058 Montliev
High Point, N. C.

Neal, Vance Brown
Route 5
Sanford, N. C.

Neighbors, Dalmo Keith
401 W. Main Street
Benson, N. C.

Neighbors, Judith Alenia
Route 1
Benson, N. C.

Nelligan, Robert Martin
Route 2, Box 94
Lynnhaven, Virginia

Newby, Max Fiddela
Route 2
Lexington, N. C.

Nobles, Don Wayne
Carolina Avenue
Washington, N. C.

Nobles, Ronald
Box 226
Richlands, N. C.

Norfleet, Leon Edgar
Smithfield, N. C.

Norris, Jimmy Austin
115 Clifton Street
Fuquay Springs, N. C.

Norris, Joseph Graham
408 N. Clinton Avenue
Dunn, N. C.

Norris, Roland Cleveland
Route 4, Box 200
Whiteville, N. C.

Norris, Terry Goal
Elizabethtown, N. C.

Norris, William Thomas, Jr.
Route 3
Raleigh, N. C.

Norton, Betty Lou
Route 2
Laurel Hill, N. C.

Oakley, Wayne Darrell
Route 1
Roxboro, N. C.

O'Berry, Walter Thomas
Evergreen, N. C.

Offutt, James Merriman
908 Rountree Road
Kinston, N. C.

Olive, David Franklin
Box 142
Four Oaks, N. C.

Olive, James E.
Route 1
Willow Springs, N. C.

Owen, George Edward
Route 2
Virgilina, Virginia

Owen, Thomas Michael
616 E. Geer Street
Durham, N. C.

Owens, Harley M., Jr.
Route 1
Dunn, N. C.

Pace, Magdline
Route 3
Lillington, N. C.

Padgette, Caroline E.
4th Street
Smithfield, N. C.

Page, Faith Helen
Route 3
Lillington, N. C.

Parker, Bobby Eugene
Route 2
Four Oaks, N. C.

Parker, David Walter
Whitakers, N. C.

Parker, Jimmy Sherrill
Box 65
Four Oaks, N. C.

Parker, Jo Ann Creech
403 West Waddel Street
Selma, N. C.

Parker, Marshlon Jean
605 South 3rd Street
Smithfield, N. C.

Parnell, Robert Harold
1808 Hamlin Street
Durham, N. C.

Parrish, Charles William
Route 2
Fuquay Springs, N. C.

Pate, Charles Blue
Rowland, N. C.

Pate, Ernest Vernon, Jr.
4444 Pimber Lane
Winston-Salem, N. C.

Patterson, Charles Wayne
1012 East Main Street
Durham, N. C.

Patterson, Daisy Ann
1402 Dixie Trail
Raleigh, N. C.

Patterson, Richard Carlton
Box 467
Sanford, N. C.

Patton, James David
1605 Crystal Lane
Greensboro, N. C.

Peacock, Don Thomas
Lake Waccamaw, N. C.

Pearce, Charles Clee, Jr.
Delano 1129
Durham, N. C.

Pearce, Clyde Pruitt
Buie's Creek, N. C.

Pearce, Priscilla Ann
Route 3
Zebulon, N. C.

Peele, Julian Thomas
1021 Lejeune Boulevard
Jacksonville, N. C.

Pender, Holice Edwin
Route 3
Four Oaks, N. C.

Pennington, Eddie Ross
2709 Newbold Street
Raleigh, N. C.

Penny, Jo Carol
Route 1
Coats, N. C.

Perry, Gaylord Jackson
Route 1, Box 176
Jamesville, N. C.

Perry, James Evan
Route 1
Williamston, N. C.

Phillips, Ann Cook
Goldston, N. C.

Phillips, Charles Larry
Goldston, N. C.

Phillips, Claude Douglas
Route 2
Raleigh, N. C.

Phipps, Jeannette
Route 5
Lumberton, N. C.

Pickett, John Samuel
500 Woodbrook
High Point, N. C.

Pierce, Horace Abhue, III
116 Bishop Street
Beckley, West Virginia

Pleasant, Jerry Thomas
Route 1
Angier, N. C.

Plummer, Joseph Ted
3516 Patricia Drive
Fayetteville, N. C.

Poe, Albert H.
2618 Nation Avenue
Durham, N. C.

Polk, Glenn Eldon, Jr.
310 Elder Lane
Fayetteville, N. C.

Pope, Jimmie Ray
111 Broughton Street
Garner, N. C.

Pope, Lloyd Busbee, III
701 West Pope
Dunn, N. C.

Pope, Rebecca Ann
Route 1
Coats, N. C.

Porter, Clayton Henderson
Route 1, Box 1 B
Lillington, N. C.

Porter, Raymond Nixon
Carthage Highway
Sanford, N. C.

Powell, Carl Flay, Sr.
423 South Front Street
Wilmington, N. C.

Powell, Samuel Fletcher
400 Penny Street
Garner, N. C.

Powers, John Duncan
Route 1
Lumberton, N. C.

Prescott, Jerry Holton
Route 1, Box 984
New Bern, N. C.

Price, Novella
Route 2
Bladenboro, N. C.

Priddy, David Andrew
405 North Pitt Street
Ayden, N. C.

Pridgen, Daphne Ann
Route 1
Fair Bluff, N. C.

Pritchard, Charles Scott
3520 Bellevue Road
Raleigh, N. C.

Pritchard, Edward Lee
200½ Dyer Street
Elizabeth City, N. C.

Purdie, Ed
603 W. Pearsell Street
Dunn, N. C.

Putnam, George Carlton
106 Clifton Road
Rocky Mount, N. C.

Quick, Gerald Gilbert
206 High Street
McColl, S. C.

Rabon, Wayne Levon
509 East 9th Street
Lumberton, N. C.

Ramsey, Harvey Goodwin
504 West Lenoir
Kinston, N. C.

Ramsey, Kader Roy
Route 1
Jacksonville, N. C.

Raynor, Elizabeth Ann
1705 Trail 5
Burlington, N. C.

Raynor, Linda Jane
105 South Elm Avenue
Dunn, N. C.

Reavis, June Ben
511 Huske Street
Fayetteville, N. C.

Reddick, Elizabeth Jeanne
6001 Hampton Blvd.
Norfolk, Virginia

Redmon, Donald Shaw
Route 1
Liberty, N. C.

Reeves, Raymond Wilson
123 Main Street
Westernport, Maryland

Register, Edwin Lee, Jr.
Route 2
Rose Hill, N. C.

Register, James Lewis
Route 3
Four Oaks, N. C.

Register, Jimmie Lee
1104 Bright Street
Kinston, N. C.

Reid, William Stanley
Peachtree Street
Rocky Mount, N. C.

Reinhardt, Clifford Jackson
Hamptonville, N. C.

Renfrow, Hilton Vester
Route 2
Kenly, N. C.

Reuschling, Gordon Nelson, Jr.
4021 Race Street
Portsmouth, Virginia

Revels, Bobby Joe
Route 2
Fuquay Springs, N. C.

Rich, Elizabeth Parker
Box 305
Burgaw, N. C.

Richards, Robert Reynold
813 Green Street
Durham, N. C.

Richman, Dave Reid
Box 9604
Raleigh, N. C.

Riddick, Janie Sue
Alliance, N. C.

Riggs, Aubrey Grant
Route 1
Hubert, N. C.

Rigsbee, Charles Stewart
1923 Ward Street
Durham, N. C.

Rigsbee, John A.
2904 Monroe Avenue
Durham, N. C.

Riley, James Rhett
College St.
Wallace, N. C.

Rinaldi, Robert Rosario
1410 Raeford Road
Fayetteville, N. C.

Rinker, Ronnie McFall
Box 1026
Stuart, Florida

Rivenbark, Robert Turner
South Rail Road
Wallace, N. C.

Rivenbark, Walter Murphy, III
Wallace, N. C.

Roberson, Bob Paul
28 Ives Street
Vallejo, California

Roberson, Jerry Watts
Box 939
Wilson, N. C.

Roberts, Carol Joanne
South 8th Street
Lebanon, Pennsylvania

Roberts, Darrel Gene
Spring Lake, N. C.

Roberts, Euette Martin, Jr.
Route 1
Broadway, N. C.

Roberts, Mary Elizabeth
2224 Circle
Raleigh, N. C.

Rogers, Linda Dare
Route 4
Roxboro, N. C.

Rogers, Reid Reginald
Buie's Creek, N. C.

Rogers, William Henry, Jr.
Route 2
Fuquay Springs, N. C.

Rogers, William Lumas
Route 1
Youngsville, N. C.

Rose, Edgar Maurice, Jr.
211 South 3rd Street
Smithfield, N. C.

Rose, Jack Cooper
Route 3
Nashville, N. C.

Rose, Paul Cedric
Route 3, Box 73
Goldsboro, N. C.

Rose, Tom
Route 1
Dudley, N. C.

Rosser, Gaither Dale
216 Helen Street
Fayetteville, N. C.

Rouse, Thomas Spencer
1315 Howard Street
Kinston, N. C.

Rowe, Bobby Gene
601 East Gordon Street
Kinston, N. C.

Rumbley, Jo Anne
1207 Marion Street
Greensboro, N. C.

Russ, Jimmy
Abbottsburg, N. C.

Sadjadi, Mahammad Mehdi Majdeh
Buie's Creek, N. C.

Salisbury, Paul Dean
Box 837
Spring Lake, N. C.

Sampson, Judith Gail
Route 1
Laurel Hill, N. C.

Sandy, Harold Lloyd
Buie's Creek, N. C.

Sansbury, Austin Baxter
518 Godwin Street
Lumberton, N. C.

Sasser, Kenneth Lindsey
Route 4
Whiteville, N. C.

Sawyer, Thomas Cecil
Route 1
Belcross, N. C.

Schramm, George
Co. B, 503 M. P. BN
Fort Bragg, N. C.

Scoggins, Billy Ordell
Route 1
Godwin, N. C.

Scripture, Murray Hobart
Fisher Street
Morehead City, N. C.

Seagroves, Norman Miller
116 South Driver Avenue
Durham, N. C.

Sercy, Jerry Davis
Route 4
Dunn, N. C.

Sexton, Ruth Blair
Route 1
Lillington, N. C.

Shelley, Henry Grady, Jr.
Route 3
Marion, S. C.

Shepard, Willie, Jr.
Wallace, N. C.

Sherman, Phyllis Anne
Route 1
Holly Springs, N. C.

Shingleton, James Ronnie
Stantonsburg, N. C.

Shreve, David Prentiss
6520 Charles Street
Falls Church, Virginia

Simpson, Douglas Jackson
1907 Fisher Street
Morehead City, N. C.

Simpson, Weldon Ervin
405 North Weble Street
Selma, N. C.

Singletary, Jerry Lane
751 Westover Boulevard
Elizabeth City, N. C.

Small, John Calvin
Box 223
Buie's Creek, N. C.

Smith, Agnes Ann
Box 42
Grimesland, N. C.

Smith, Frances Ringgold
1105 Johnston Street
Greenville, N. C.

Smith, Gery Douglas
1427 Canterbury Road
Raleigh, N. C.

Smith, Harry Rankin, Jr.
1536 Rankin Road
Greensboro, N. C.

Smith, James Hugh
517 Waldo Street
Cary, N. C.

Smith, Jesse E.
Route 2
Mount Olive, N. C.

Smith, Johnnie Mae
Bluffton, South Carolina

Smith, Philip Dewar
Route 2
Fuquay Springs, N. C.

Snell, Daphne Kay
Route 2, Box 131
Roper, N. C.

Snider, Lloyd Butner
Mendenhall Trailer Court
Route 1
Cary, N. C.

Snipes, Charles L.
211 South Racford Street
Selma, N. C.

Snow, William Hale
Stuart, Florida

Snyder, Daniel Holland
208 Jones Franklin
Raleigh, N. C.

Sodergren, Kenneth White
112 West End Boulevard
Emporia, Virginia

Soles, Richard Vernon, Jr.
Route 4
Whiteville, N. C.

Spalding, H. Daniel
4208 7th Avenue
Landover Hills, Maryland

Spell, Albert Charles
Box 213
Hope Mills, N. C.

Spell, William Earl
Route 1
Autryville, N. C.

Spencer, John William
1300 Virginia Avenue
Durham, N. C.

Spender, William Edward
Route 2
Burgaw, N. C.

Spivey, Orin Ralph, Jr.
Box 111
Roseboro, N. C.

Spivey, Thomas Averette
Roseboro, N. C.

Stafford, Charles Lewis
Route 4
Dunn, N. C.

Stallings, Arthur Whitt
Route 1
Raleigh, N. C.

Stanley, Hubert Currie, Jr.
2311 Market Street
Wilmington, N. C.

Stanley, Larry Monroe
Route 1
Clarendon, N. C.

Starling, James Alton, Jr.
Box 5
Pinelevel, N. C.

Starling, Mary Stevens
315 Oak Hill Drive
Emporia, Virginia

Steele, Edouard Besson
203 North Blount Street
Raleigh, N. C.

Steinberg, David Ronald
211 East "H" Street
Erwin, N. C.

Stephens, Annie Laura
Box 174
Fairmont, N. C.

Stephens, Edna Sessoms
Erwin, N. C.

Stephens, John Lee
Route 2
Lillington, N. C.

Stephens, Rebecca Anne
209 East "F" Street
Erwin, N. C.

Stephens, William Jones
407 South 17 Street
Erwin, N. C.

Stephenson, Alton Louis, Jr.
204 East "E" Street
Erwin, N. C.

Stephenson, Jackie Hooks
Route 1, Box 362
Clayton, N. C.

Stephenson, Thomas Williams
600 West Main Street
Benson, N. C.

Stevens, Jerry Hughes
1416 Dixie Trail
Raleigh, N. C.

Stewart, Barbara Lynne
Route 1
Coats, N. C.

Stewart, Bella Mae
Mamers, N. C.

Stewart, Cyrus Franklin
Lillington, N. C.

Stewart, Kermit Harold
Lillington, N. C.

Stewart, Theodosia Ivey
Route 3, Box 230
Goldsboro, N. C.

Stokes, Howard Austin
200 South Cherry Grove Avenue
Annapolis, Maryland

Stone, Eleanore Ruth
325 East Trinity Street
Durham, N. C.

Storey, Lorraine A
Route 1
Murfreesboro, N. C.

Stout, James Buron
1308 13th Street
Lillington, N. C.

Stribling, Casper Eugene
1002 McKellar Drive
Tullahoma, Tennessee

Strickland, Addie Jo
Route 1
Fair Bluff, N. C.

Strickland, Anna Neal
Cerro Gordo, N. C.

Strickland, Bernice Leslie
114 East Lee Street
Zebulon, N. C.

Strickland, Deloit
803 South Magnolia Avenue
Dunn, N. C.

Strickland, James Harper
311 W. Waddell Street
Selma, N. C.

Strickland, Jancie Grey
504 Cutchin Street
Clinton, N. C.

Strickland, Jess Willard
Route 1
Fair Bluff, N. C.

Strickland, Paul Graham
505 South 16th Street
Erwin, N. C.

Strickland, Thomas Kay
413 South Magnolia
Dunn, N. C.

Strickland, Wayne McCoy
Route 3
Mount Olive, N. C.

Stubbs, Daphne Ann
Route 5
Lumberton, N. C.

Sullivan, Britt Everett
1605 Sunrise Avenue
Raleigh, N. C.

Sullivan, Joe Warren
Route 3
Carthage, N. C.

Sullivan, Vernon Ray
Route 1
Selma, N. C.

Sumrell, John R.
Harbinger, N. C.

Sutton, Wellington Patton, Jr.
Box 204
Lillington, N. C.

Swain, Jeanette Gayle
917 Curtis Street
Ahoskie, N. C.

Swanson, Jerry Floyd
Route 7, Box 59
Fayetteville, N. C.

Sweum, Miriam Gertrude
Route 3
Whiteville, N. C.

Sykes, Clyde Deward
Route 4
Louisburg, N. C.

Tarlton, Ethel Lorraine
5347 E. Lakeside Drive
Raleigh, N. C.

Tart, Delorah Mae
Route 2
Lillington, N. C.

Tart, Lewis Newton
Route 2
Dunn, N. C.

Tate, Charles Lacy
Chadbourn, N. C.

Taylor, Mrs. Gertrude B
Box 123
Angier, N. C.

Taylor, Jessie Allison
Route 1
Wilson, N. C.

Taylor, Joe G.
409 Line Avenue
Greenville, N. C.

Taylor, John Preston
Box 3266
Fayetteville, N. C.

Taylor, Stephanie Merritt
309 E. E Street
Erwin, N. C.

Taylor, Sue Katherine
Route 2
Zebulon, N. C.

Telfair, Richard Badger
211 Hawthorne Road
Raleigh, N. C.

Temple, Tommy Hoyle
Zebulon, N. C.

Terrell, Alva Lee
1107 Hargrove Street
Henderson, N. C.

Terrell, Andrew Page
1107 Hargrove Street
Henderson, N. C.

Tew, Charles Lynwood
508 N. McKay Avenue
Dunn, N. C.

Thames, William Glenn
Hope Mills, N. C.

Thigpen, John Marvin
P. O. Box 93
Mount Olive, N. C.

Thomas, John Mitchell
203 Ashe Street
Bladenboro, N. C.

Thomas, Johnsie Elizabeth
1784 Jameston Drive
Charlotte 9, N. C.

Thompson, Gene Elliott
King Street
Elizabethtown, N. C.

Thompson, Margaret Christine
103 N. Madison Street
Whiteville, N. C.

Thompson, William R.
Box 88
Chapel Hill, N. C.

Thornton, Doris Jean
914 N. Third Street
Wilmington, N. C.

Thurman, Patrick Coit
718 Falls Road
Rocky Mount, N. C.

Tilghman, Granville Myers
218 W. Pearsall Street
Dunn, N. C.

Tilley, Adolphus Linwood
1000 Hammond Street
Rocky Mount, N. C.

Tilley, Kenneth Matthew
Fuquay Springs, N. C.

Tingen, Robert Wayne
411 W. Academy
Fuquay Springs, N. C.

Titmus, Edward Buford
Route 3, Box 241
Petersburg, Virginia

Todd, James William
Route 2, Box 55
Warsaw, N. C.

Trader, James Henry
6 Cheston Avenue
Annapolis, Md.

Travers, Philip Achillije
South Plymouth Street
Fayetteville, N. C.

Tripp, Betty Jo
Buie's Creek, N. C.

Tripp, William Burton
315 E. Third Street
Ayden, N. C.

Truelove, Jerry C.
602 Sasser Street
Raleigh, N. C.

Turlington, June Dare
111 East G Street
Erwin, N. C.

Turner, Robert W.
Route 3, Box 571
Raleigh, N. C.

Turner, William Herbert
508 West Main Street
Ahoskie, N. C.

Tuttle, Linda Helen
4401 Colonial Avenue
Norfolk, Virginia

Twiford, Louis Brason
1200 Jones Avenue
Elizabeth City, N. C.

Tyndall, Carl Haywood
Route 1
Pikeville, N. C.

Tysinger, Jerry Raymond
619 Martha Street
High Point, N. C.

Utley, Phil Thomas
623 Cape Fear Avenue
Fayetteville, N. C.

Vanaman, Robert Frederick
802 Ethclored
Fayetteville, N. C.

Vann, Harriette Elizabeth
E. Church Street
Benson, N. C.

Vaughn, James Graham
Route 4, Box 15
Fayetteville, N. C.

Vaughan, Victoria Elizabeth
Route 1, Box 417
Durham, N. C.

Vaughn, Marie
216 Elm Street
Raleigh, N. C.

Vaughn, Robert Lee
216 Elm Street
Raleigh, N. C.

Vest, Janice Gayle
Box 52
Red Springs, N. C.

Vincent, Alton Gene
1008 Colonial Avenue
Greenville, N. C.

Vinson, Edward LaRue
2101 Providence Road
Charlotte, N. C.

Vinson, Leonard R.
105 E. Whitaker Mill
Raleigh, N. C.

Wade, Walter Mack, Jr.
Route 1
Lillington, N. C.

Wagnon, Brenda Magdeline
2747 Layten Avenue
Raleigh, N. C.

Walker, Ralph Edwin
Ridgeway, Virginia

Walker, Samuel Archie, Jr.
Sligo, N. C.

Wallace, Edmond Clayton
2618 Hillsboro Road
Durham, N. C.

Wallace, Richard Bruce
Route 1
Cerro Gordo, N. C.

Walters, William Cecil
Route 3
Oxford, N. C.

Walters, William Johnson
244 West 75th Street
New York, New York

Ward, Carr Monroe
201 West 2nd Avenue
Lexington, N. C.

Ward, Thomas D.
Route 1
Aynor, S. C.

Warren, Allen Joseph
Route 5, Box 400
Clinton, N. C.

Warren, Janet Rose
Route 1
Dunn, N. C.

Warren, Patricia Anne
115 Adams Street
Durham, N. C.

Washer, Robert James
Merrick, New York

Waters, Rubylene
Route 1
Mount Olive, N. C.

Watkins, George Thomas
218 Park Avenue
Raleigh, N. C.

Watson, Betsy Jean
Gen. Delivery
Ingold, N. C.

Watson, James Purdie
Moncure, N. C.

Wayburn, Sam Morris
2708 Fairview Road
Raleigh, N. C.

Wayland, Bruce Fowler
Rock Spring Road
Wake Forest, N. C.

Weaver, Dyal Jean
307 North 11th Street
Erwin, N. C.

Webster, Frances Rebecca
Route 2
Madison, N. C.

Weddle, Roberte Lee
Buie's Creek, N. C.

Wells, James Wynn
Roseboro, N. C.

Wells, Juanita Inez
Box 29
Harrells, N. C.

Wells, Nancy Dallas
Teachey, N. C.

Welsh, Kenneth Gordon, Jr.
1606 Pineview Street
Raleigh, N. C.

West, Ethel Stokes
Route 1
Linden, N. C.

West, James Alderman
Route 1, Box 149
Aberdeen, N. C.

West, Percy White, Jr.
306 Bracken
Sanford, N. C.

West, Wallace Ray
Route 1
Dunn, N. C.

Whaley, Carole Annette
Route 3
Kinston, N. C.

Wheless, Edith Gray
Route 1
Franklin, N. C.

Whitaker, William Jeb, Jr.
Route 1
Youngsville, N. C.

Whitby, Herman Wesley
902 Rapids Street
Roanoke Rapids, N. C.

White, Beverly Mae
Route 1, Box 353
Youngsville, N. C.

White, Eleanor Kay
Route 3
Elizabeth City, N. C.

White, Raymond Marshall
P. O. Box 547
Bartow, Florida

Whitley, James Robert
Main Street
Woodland, N. C.

Wiggins, June Gail
414 Lafayette Street
Clinton, N. C.

Wilder, Jerry Jane
Route 1
Middlesex, N. C.

Wiles, Jim Ravine
Route 2
North Wilkesboro, N. C.

Wilkinson, Lillian Eugenia
831 Wilkerson Avenue
Durham, N. C.

Willard, Robert Wayne
Cleveland Avenue
Riverside, New Jersey

Williams, Albert Edwin
Route 1
Smithfield, N. C.

Williams, Bess Jane
O'Niel Street
Clayton, N. C.

Williams, Erma Gray
Route 3
Four Oaks, N. C.

Williams, Hooper Luther
Buie's Creek, N. C.

Williams, Howard Eugene, Jr.
5251 Waterman Blvd.
St. Louis, Missouri

Williams, John P., Jr.
Route 2
Roseboro, N. C.

Williams, Junius Sneed
203 Sutton Street
Fayetteville, N. C.

Williams, Lois Revine
Route 2
Pink Hill, N. C.

Williams, Stanley Owen
Route 3
Wake Forest, N. C.

Williams, Susan Ann
Route 1
Newton Grove, N. C.

Williamson, Stephen Monroe
Box 254
Kenansville, N. C.

Williford, Peggy Ann
2209 Morganton Road
Fayetteville, N. C.

Williford, Sonja Lee
Sanders Street
Maxton, N. C.

Wilson, Carolyn Wray
Rocky Point, N. C.

Wilson, Donald
Route 1
Bunnlevel, N. C.

Wilson, Elizabeth Rose
Route 2
Whiteville, N. C.

Wilson, Sara Frances
Route 2
Angier, N. C.

Wimberly, Patricia Ann
Route 1
Lillington, N. C.

Womack, Buck J.
Route 1
Broadway, N. C.

Womble, Russell Barnhardt
539 Summitt Drive
Sanford, N. C.

Wood, Benny Burton
607 N. Orange Avenue
Dunn, N. C.

Wood, Earl E.
Box 13
Mamers, N. C.

Wood, Jack Franklin
Box 23
Lillington, N. C.

Wood, Judy Faye
611 W. Broad Street
Dunn, N. C.

Woodard, Louis Herman
107 E. Washington
Kinston, N. C.

Woodard, Mary Craig
110 N. George Street
Goldsboro, N. C.

Woodley, Dora Hesta
Angier, N. C.

Wortham, James H.
Route 1
Fuquay Springs, N. C.

Wright, Joe Woodruff
Hamptonville, N. C.

Wright, Vincent Broda
111-B Dobbin Avenue
Fayetteville, N. C.

Young, Jean R.
200 S. Orange Avenue
Dunn, N. C.

Young, Jimmie Bryant
Route 1
Louisburg, N. C.

Young, Thomas Alvey
Route 2
Woodsdale, N. C.

FACULTY AND STAFF

Campbell, Dr. Leslie H.
Buie's Creek, N. C.

Allen, Howard E.
2912 McCalla Avenue
Knoxville, Tennessee

Bagby, Mrs. A. Paul
Buie's Creek, N. C.

Bain, Harold C.
203 N. Orange Avenue
Dunn, N. C.

Barber, Miss Barbara
Box 282
Buie's Creek, N. C.

Barry, Lynn
Buie's Creek, N. C.

Blackmon, Dr. Bruce B.
Buie's Creek, N. C.

Bond, Mr. and Mrs. J. Nurney
Buie's Creek, N. C.

Britton, Mrs. George
Dunn, N. C.

Burkot, Mr. and Mrs. A. R.
Buie's Creek, N. C.

Cansler, Miss Ora C.
Route 4, Box 73
Wilson, N. C.

Caudell, F. M.
Box 362
Buie's Creek, N. C.

Clifton, J. Malcolm
Kelly, N. C.

Collins, Tom
Mullens, S. C.

Currin, Robert
Buie's Creek, N. C.

Davis, Mrs. Carl
Route 1
Lillington, N. C.

Davis, Mr. and Mrs. Hargrove
3731 S. Front Street
Wilmington, N. C.

Davis, Leon
Buie's Creek, N. C.

Edwards, Dr. Martha E.
507 N. 6th Avenue
Portsmouth, Virginia

Eubanks, Mrs. Ethel
205 Watts Street
Durham, N. C.

Faison, Mr. and Mrs. James L.
Buie's Creek, N. C.

Gass, W. Conard
Buie's Creek, N. C.

Gilbert, Mrs. Tom
410 General Lee Avenue
Dunn, N. C.

Godwin, Mrs. Cecilia
Box 293
Dunn, N. C.

Graham, George S.
243 Park Avenue
Lundlow, Ky.

Gregory, Mrs. Clyde
Buie's Creek, N. C.

Griffin, Miss Jessie C.
503 W. Harnett Street
Dunn, N. C.

Holt, Mrs. Ralph
Buie's Creek, N. C.

Hopson, Mrs. Emma Lee
Buie's Creek, N. C.

Horton, Mr. and Mrs. Charles A.
400 S. Mercer Street
Bluefield, W. Virginia

Howard, Rev. Charles
Buie's Creek, N. C.

Jenkins, Mr. and Mrs. B. W.
Buie's Creek, N. C.

Johnson, Rev. E. Weldon
Buie's Creek, N. C.

Jones, Allen
Buie's Creek, N. C.

Kennedy, Mr. and Mrs. Philip
1244 Gilmore Lane
Louisville, Ky.

King, Robert
Buie's Creek, N. C.

Langston, Dr. Perry Q.
Box 257
Buie's Creek, N. C.

Lasater, Mrs. E. H., Sr.
Route 1
Erwin, N. C.

Lasater, Mrs. Eugene, Jr.
Route 1
Erwin, N. C.

Lloyd, Mrs. Carl
Buie's Creek, N. C.

Lockwood, David
18 Aster Drive
De Bary, Florida

Lynch, Mrs. A. E.
Buie's Creek, N. C.

McCall, Fred
Buie's Creek, N. C.

Matthews, Mrs. M. B., Jr.
Buie's Creek, N. C.

Mix, Miss Charlotte
Box 625
Dover, Delaware

Morgan, Mrs. Robert H.
Buie's Creek, N. C.

Nelson, E. L.
Buie's Creek, N. C.

Newton, Robert Lee
Buie's Creek, N. C.

Pearce, Mrs. Clyde
Buie's Creek, N. C.

Perkins, Miss Geraldine
1539 Wildwood Avenue
Columbus, Georgia

Phelps, Don
Box 65
Creswell, N. C.

Phelps, Herman
Buie's Creek, N. C.

Powell, Miss Mabel
Buie's Creek, N. C.

Powell, Miss Nell
Buie's Creek, N. C.

Proffit, Mrs. G. T.
Lillington, N. C.

Ragland, Mrs. Jack
Buie's Creek, N. C.

Ragland, Miss Mary Susan
Buie's Creek, N. C.

Rogers, Mr. and Mrs. Dewey
Buie's Creek, N. C.

Rutherford, Thomas C.
4111 Trenholm Road
Columbia, S. C.

Sadler, Mrs. Inez G.
Box 117, S. L. I.
Lafayette, Louisiana

Small, Mr. and Mrs. Lonnie
Buie's Creek, N. C.

Smith, Mrs. Jessie
Buie's Creek, N. C.

Sorensen, Roald H.
Buie's Creek, N. C.

Stephens, Mrs. Edna
209 East F Street
Erwin, N. C.

Stewart, Ashley
Buie's Creek, N. C.

Swann, Mrs. George
Buie's Creek, N. C.

Thompson, Dr. John G.
Box 233
Buie's Creek, N. C.

Tripp, Mr. and Mrs. G. A.
Buie's Creek, N. C.

Tripp, Miss Yvonne
700 Fairground Road
Dunn, N. C.

Tuck, Mr. and Mrs. William P.
Box 277
Buie's Creek, N. C.

Tuttle, Alan
3508 Starmount Drive
Greensboro, N. C.

Walker, E. M.
Buie's Creek, N. C.

White, Mary Jane
10 Maple Road
Concord, N. C.

AUTOGRAPHS

AUTOGRAPHS

Lightning Source UK Ltd.
Milton Keynes UK
UKHW051116210820
368606UK00011B/820